Applications Infrastructure Complete Self-Assessment Guide

The guidance in this Self-Assessment is base
Infrastructure best practices and standards i
architecture, design and quality managemei
on the professional judgment of the individu
Acknowledgments.

Notice of rights

Trademarks

Table of Contents

4

About The Art of Service

The Art of Service, Business Process Architects since 2000, is dedicated to helping stakeholders achieve excellence.

Defining, designing, creating, and implementing a process to solve a stakeholders challenge or meet an objective is the most valuable role… In EVERY group, company, organization and department.

Unless you're talking a one-time, single-use project, there should be a process. Whether that process is managed and implemented by humans, AI, or a combination of the two, it needs to be designed by someone with a complex enough perspective to ask the right questions.

Someone capable of asking the right questions and step back and say, 'What are we really trying to accomplish here? And is there a different way to look at it?'

With The Art of Service's Standard Requirements Self-Assessments, we empower people who can do just that — whether their title is marketer, entrepreneur, manager, salesperson, consultant, Business Process Manager, executive assistant, IT Manager, CIO etc... —they are the people who rule the future. They are people who watch the process as it happens, and ask the right questions to make the process work better.

Contact us when you need any support with this Self-Assessment and any help with templates, blue-prints and examples of standard documents you might need:

http://theartofservice.com
service@theartofservice.com

Included Resources - how to access

Included with your purchase of the book is the Applications

Infrastructure Self-Assessment Spreadsheet Dashboard which contains all questions and Self-Assessment areas and auto-generates insights, graphs, and project RACI planning - all with examples to get you started right away.

How? Simply send an email to
access@theartofservice.com
with this books' title in the subject to get the
Applications Infrastructure Self Assessment Tool right
away.

You will receive the following contents with New and Updated specific criteria:

• The latest quick edition of the book in PDF

• The latest complete edition of the book in PDF, which criteria correspond to the criteria in...

• The Self-Assessment Excel Dashboard, and...

• Example pre-filled Self-Assessment Excel Dashboard to get familiar with results generation

• In-depth specific Checklists covering the topic

• Project management checklists and templates to assist with implementation

INCLUDES LIFETIME SELF ASSESSMENT UPDATES

Every self assessment comes with Lifetime Updates and Lifetime Free Updated Books. Lifetime Updates is an industry-first feature which allows you to receive verified self assessment updates, ensuring you always have the most accurate information at your fingertips.

Get it now- you will be glad you did - do it now, before you forget.

Send an email to **access@theartofservice.com** with this books' title in the subject to get the Applications Infrastructure Self Assessment Tool right away.

Purpose of this Self-Assessment

This Self-Assessment has been developed to improve understanding of the requirements and elements of Applications Infrastructure, based on best practices and standards in business process architecture, design and quality management.

It is designed to allow for a rapid Self-Assessment to determine how closely existing management practices and procedures correspond to the elements of the Self-Assessment.

The criteria of requirements and elements of Applications Infrastructure have been rephrased in the format of a Self-Assessment questionnaire, with a seven-criterion scoring system, as explained in this document.

In this format, even with limited background knowledge of Applications Infrastructure, a manager can quickly review existing operations to determine how they measure up to the standards. This in turn can serve as the starting point of a 'gap analysis' to identify management tools or system elements that might usefully be implemented in the organization to help improve overall performance.

How to use the Self-Assessment

On the following pages are a series of questions to identify to what extent your Applications Infrastructure initiative is complete in comparison to the requirements set in standards.

To facilitate answering the questions, there is a space in front of each question to enter a score on a scale of '1' to '5'.

> 1 Strongly Disagree
>
> 2 Disagree
>
> 3 Neutral
>
> 4 Agree
>
> 5 Strongly Agree

Read the question and rate it with the following in front of mind:

'In my belief,
the answer to this question is clearly defined'.

There are two ways in which you can choose to interpret this statement;
1. how aware are you that the answer to the question is clearly defined
2. for more in-depth analysis you can choose to gather evidence and confirm the answer to the question. This obviously will take more time, most Self-Assessment users opt for the first way to interpret the question and dig deeper later on based on the outcome of the overall Self-Assessment.

A score of '1' would mean that the answer is not clear at all, where a '5' would mean the answer is crystal clear and defined. Leave emtpy when the question is not applicable or you don't want to answer it, you can skip it without affecting your score. Write your score in the space provided.

After you have responded to all the appropriate statements in each section, compute your average score for that section, using the formula provided, and round to the nearest tenth. Then transfer to the corresponding spoke in the Applications Infrastructure Scorecard on the second next page of the Self-Assessment.

Your completed Applications Infrastructure Scorecard will give you a clear presentation of which Applications Infrastructure areas need attention.

Applications Infrastructure Scorecard Example

Example of how the finalized Scorecard can look like:

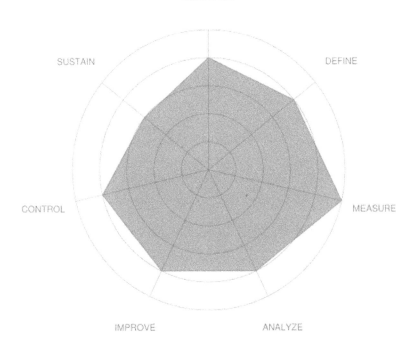

Applications Infrastructure Scorecard

Your Scores:

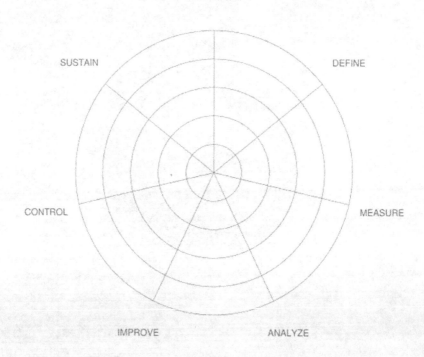

BEGINNING OF THE SELF-ASSESSMENT:

CRITERION #1: RECOGNIZE

INTENT: Be aware of the need for change. Recognize that there is an unfavorable variation, problem or symptom.

In my belief, the answer to this question is clearly defined:

5 Strongly Agree

4 Agree

3 Neutral

2 Disagree

1 Strongly Disagree

1. Consider your own Applications Infrastructure project, what types of organizational problems do you think might be causing or affecting your problem, based on the work done so far?
<--- Score

2. Are there any specific expectations or concerns about the Applications Infrastructure team, Applications Infrastructure itself?

<--- Score

3. Why the need?
<--- Score

4. What vendors make products that address the Applications Infrastructure needs?
<--- Score

5. What is the Applications Infrastructure problem definition? What do you need to resolve?
<--- Score

6. Do you need to avoid or amend any Applications Infrastructure activities?
<--- Score

7. What are the expected benefits of Applications Infrastructure to the stakeholder?
<--- Score

8. Are there any revenue recognition issues?
<--- Score

9. What extra resources will you need?
<--- Score

10. What Applications Infrastructure capabilities do you need?
<--- Score

11. What activities does the governance board need to consider?
<--- Score

12. Are there Applications Infrastructure problems

defined?
<--- Score

13. How are training requirements identified?
<--- Score

14. Where do you need to exercise leadership?
<--- Score

15. How do you assess your Applications Infrastructure workforce capability and capacity needs, including skills, competencies, and staffing levels?
<--- Score

16. Are employees recognized for desired behaviors?
<--- Score

17. What is the extent or complexity of the Applications Infrastructure problem?
<--- Score

18. What should be considered when identifying available resources, constraints, and deadlines?
<--- Score

19. What are the stakeholder objectives to be achieved with Applications Infrastructure?
<--- Score

20. Will Applications Infrastructure deliverables need to be tested and, if so, by whom?
<--- Score

21. What are the minority interests and what amount of minority interests can be recognized?

<--- Score

22. What is the recognized need?
<--- Score

23. Think about the people you identified for your Applications Infrastructure project and the project responsibilities you would assign to them, what kind of training do you think they would need to perform these responsibilities effectively?
<--- Score

24. Is the quality assurance team identified?
<--- Score

25. Can management personnel recognize the monetary benefit of Applications Infrastructure?
<--- Score

26. Would you recognize a threat from the inside?
<--- Score

27. Does your organization need more Applications Infrastructure education?
<--- Score

28. What resources or support might you need?
<--- Score

29. What is the smallest subset of the problem you can usefully solve?
<--- Score

30. Who else hopes to benefit from it?
<--- Score

31. What prevents you from making the changes you know will make you a more effective Applications Infrastructure leader?
<--- Score

32. Looking at each person individually – does every one have the qualities which are needed to work in this group?
<--- Score

33. How does it fit into your organizational needs and tasks?
<--- Score

34. Is the need for organizational change recognized?
<--- Score

35. Are there regulatory / compliance issues?
<--- Score

36. How much are sponsors, customers, partners, stakeholders involved in Applications Infrastructure? In other words, what are the risks, if Applications Infrastructure does not deliver successfully?
<--- Score

37. Is it needed?
<--- Score

38. What would happen if Applications Infrastructure weren't done?
<--- Score

39. What Applications Infrastructure coordination do you need?
<--- Score

40. Are your goals realistic? Do you need to redefine your problem? Perhaps the problem has changed or maybe you have reached your goal and need to set a new one?

<--- Score

41. Who should resolve the Applications Infrastructure issues?

<--- Score

42. Which issues are too important to ignore?

<--- Score

43. Whom do you really need or want to serve?

<--- Score

44. How do you recognize an objection?

<--- Score

45. What are the clients issues and concerns?

<--- Score

46. Have you identified your Applications Infrastructure key performance indicators?

<--- Score

47. Which information does the Applications Infrastructure business case need to include?

<--- Score

48. How can auditing be a preventative security measure?

<--- Score

49. Does the problem have ethical dimensions?

<--- Score

50. Who defines the rules in relation to any given issue?
<--- Score

51. What are your needs in relation to Applications Infrastructure skills, labor, equipment, and markets?
<--- Score

52. Are employees recognized or rewarded for performance that demonstrates the highest levels of integrity?
<--- Score

53. What are the timeframes required to resolve each of the issues/problems?
<--- Score

54. Are problem definition and motivation clearly presented?
<--- Score

55. What Applications Infrastructure problem should be solved?
<--- Score

56. What needs to stay?
<--- Score

57. What do employees need in the short term?
<--- Score

58. To what extent does each concerned units management team recognize Applications Infrastructure as an effective investment?

<--- Score

59. Who are your key stakeholders who need to sign off?
<--- Score

60. Are there recognized Applications Infrastructure problems?
<--- Score

61. Who needs to know about Applications Infrastructure?
<--- Score

62. Do you know what you need to know about Applications Infrastructure?
<--- Score

63. Will a response program recognize when a crisis occurs and provide some level of response?
<--- Score

64. Will it solve real problems?
<--- Score

65. Is it clear when you think of the day ahead of you what activities and tasks you need to complete?
<--- Score

66. Are you dealing with any of the same issues today as yesterday? What can you do about this?
<--- Score

67. How are the Applications Infrastructure's objectives aligned to the group's overall stakeholder strategy?

<--- Score

68. As a sponsor, customer or management, how important is it to meet goals, objectives?
<--- Score

69. Who needs to know?
<--- Score

70. What problems are you facing and how do you consider Applications Infrastructure will circumvent those obstacles?
<--- Score

71. What creative shifts do you need to take?
<--- Score

72. What information do users need?
<--- Score

73. Are controls defined to recognize and contain problems?
<--- Score

74. What is the problem or issue?
<--- Score

75. Does Applications Infrastructure create potential expectations in other areas that need to be recognized and considered?
<--- Score

76. Who needs budgets?
<--- Score

77. What else needs to be measured?

<--- Score

78. What do you need to start doing?
<--- Score

79. Do you need different information or graphics?
<--- Score

80. What does Applications Infrastructure success mean to the stakeholders?
<--- Score

81. What tools and technologies are needed for a custom Applications Infrastructure project?
<--- Score

82. What are the Applications Infrastructure resources needed?
<--- Score

83. Did you miss any major Applications Infrastructure issues?
<--- Score

84. Will new equipment/products be required to facilitate Applications Infrastructure delivery, for example is new software needed?
<--- Score

85. How do you recognize an Applications Infrastructure objection?
<--- Score

86. Who needs what information?
<--- Score

87. How are you going to measure success?
<--- Score

88. How do you take a forward-looking perspective in identifying Applications Infrastructure research related to market response and models?
<--- Score

89. What is the problem and/or vulnerability?
<--- Score

90. How many trainings, in total, are needed?
<--- Score

91. What Applications Infrastructure events should you attend?
<--- Score

92. How do you identify the kinds of information that you will need?
<--- Score

93. For your Applications Infrastructure project, identify and describe the business environment, is there more than one layer to the business environment?
<--- Score

94. Do you recognize Applications Infrastructure achievements?
<--- Score

95. Do you have/need 24-hour access to key personnel?
<--- Score

96. Where is training needed?
<--- Score

97. Which needs are not included or involved?
<--- Score

98. What needs to be done?
<--- Score

99. Are losses recognized in a timely manner?
<--- Score

100. What situation(s) led to this Applications Infrastructure Self Assessment?
<--- Score

101. How do you identify subcontractor relationships?
<--- Score

Add up total points for this section:
_ _ _ _ _ = Total points for this section

Divided by: _ _ _ _ _ _ (number of statements answered) = _ _ _ _ _ _
Average score for this section

Transfer your score to the Applications Infrastructure Index at the beginning of the Self-Assessment.

CRITERION #2: DEFINE:

INTENT: Formulate the stakeholder problem. Define the problem, needs and objectives.

In my belief, the answer to this question is clearly defined:

5 Strongly Agree

4 Agree

3 Neutral

2 Disagree

1 Strongly Disagree

1. When is the estimated completion date?
<--- Score

2. What knowledge or experience is required?
<--- Score

3. What information do you gather?
<--- Score

4. Have the customer needs been translated into specific, measurable requirements? How?
<--- Score

5. Have all basic functions of Applications Infrastructure been defined?
<--- Score

6. What is in scope?
<--- Score

7. Have specific policy objectives been defined?
<--- Score

8. How do you gather Applications Infrastructure requirements?
<--- Score

9. What information should you gather?
<--- Score

10. How do you build the right business case?
<--- Score

11. What baselines are required to be defined and managed?
<--- Score

12. Has a team charter been developed and communicated?
<--- Score

13. What is the definition of Applications Infrastructure excellence?
<--- Score

14. What is the scope of the Applications Infrastructure work?
<--- Score

15. Has a high-level 'as is' process map been completed, verified and validated?
<--- Score

16. Are there any constraints known that bear on the ability to perform Applications Infrastructure work? How is the team addressing them?
<--- Score

17. Will a Applications Infrastructure production readiness review be required?
<--- Score

18. Has the Applications Infrastructure work been fairly and/or equitably divided and delegated among team members who are qualified and capable to perform the work? Has everyone contributed?
<--- Score

19. Is scope creep really all bad news?
<--- Score

20. What is the definition of success?
<--- Score

21. How is the team tracking and documenting its work?
<--- Score

22. Do the problem and goal statements meet the SMART criteria (specific, measurable, attainable, relevant, and time-bound)?

<--- Score

23. What is out of scope?
<--- Score

24. How would you define Applications Infrastructure leadership?
<--- Score

25. Where can you gather more information?
<--- Score

26. Are required metrics defined, what are they?
<--- Score

27. When are meeting minutes sent out? Who is on the distribution list?
<--- Score

28. Is the work to date meeting requirements?
<--- Score

29. Is Applications Infrastructure required?
<--- Score

30. What is a worst-case scenario for losses?
<--- Score

31. What Applications Infrastructure requirements should be gathered?
<--- Score

32. What are the Applications Infrastructure use cases?
<--- Score

33. What is the context?

<--- Score

34. Has anyone else (internal or external to the group) attempted to solve this problem or a similar one before? If so, what knowledge can be leveraged from these previous efforts?
<--- Score

35. Is there a critical path to deliver Applications Infrastructure results?
<--- Score

36. How was the 'as is' process map developed, reviewed, verified and validated?
<--- Score

37. Is the improvement team aware of the different versions of a process: what they think it is vs. what it actually is vs. what it should be vs. what it could be?
<--- Score

38. What was the context?
<--- Score

39. Who approved the Applications Infrastructure scope?
<--- Score

40. Are audit criteria, scope, frequency and methods defined?
<--- Score

41. The political context: who holds power?
<--- Score

42. Has everyone on the team, including the team

leaders, been properly trained?
<--- Score

43. Is special Applications Infrastructure user knowledge required?
<--- Score

44. What is the scope of the Applications Infrastructure effort?
<--- Score

45. Are approval levels defined for contracts and supplements to contracts?
<--- Score

46. What gets examined?
<--- Score

47. How will variation in the actual durations of each activity be dealt with to ensure that the expected Applications Infrastructure results are met?
<--- Score

48. What are the tasks and definitions?
<--- Score

49. How do you gather the stories?
<--- Score

50. What happens if Applications Infrastructure's scope changes?
<--- Score

51. What is in the scope and what is not in scope?
<--- Score

52. Is there any additional Applications Infrastructure definition of success?
<--- Score

53. Scope of sensitive information?
<--- Score

54. How often are the team meetings?
<--- Score

55. How does the Applications Infrastructure manager ensure against scope creep?
<--- Score

56. Who are the Applications Infrastructure improvement team members, including Management Leads and Coaches?
<--- Score

57. Are all requirements met?
<--- Score

58. How do you keep key subject matter experts in the loop?
<--- Score

59. Do you have organizational privacy requirements?
<--- Score

60. Why are you doing Applications Infrastructure and what is the scope?
<--- Score

61. How and when will the baselines be defined?
<--- Score

62. Are roles and responsibilities formally defined?
<--- Score

63. Do you all define Applications Infrastructure in the same way?
<--- Score

64. What are (control) requirements for Applications Infrastructure Information?
<--- Score

65. When is/was the Applications Infrastructure start date?
<--- Score

66. Is there a completed SIPOC representation, describing the Suppliers, Inputs, Process, Outputs, and Customers?
<--- Score

67. Who defines (or who defined) the rules and roles?
<--- Score

68. Are task requirements clearly defined?
<--- Score

69. Has/have the customer(s) been identified?
<--- Score

70. How have you defined all Applications Infrastructure requirements first?
<--- Score

71. Is there regularly 100% attendance at the team meetings? If not, have appointed substitutes

attended to preserve cross-functionality and full representation?

<--- Score

72. Does the scope remain the same?

<--- Score

73. Has a project plan, Gantt chart, or similar been developed/completed?

<--- Score

74. What are the compelling stakeholder reasons for embarking on Applications Infrastructure?

<--- Score

75. What are the rough order estimates on cost savings/opportunities that Applications Infrastructure brings?

<--- Score

76. How do you catch Applications Infrastructure definition inconsistencies?

<--- Score

77. What defines best in class?

<--- Score

78. What system do you use for gathering Applications Infrastructure information?

<--- Score

79. Are there different segments of customers?

<--- Score

80. Are accountability and ownership for Applications Infrastructure clearly defined?

<--- Score

81. How do you manage unclear Applications Infrastructure requirements?
<--- Score

82. Is there a completed, verified, and validated high-level 'as is' (not 'should be' or 'could be') stakeholder process map?
<--- Score

83. How do you hand over Applications Infrastructure context?
<--- Score

84. What intelligence can you gather?
<--- Score

85. Is Applications Infrastructure linked to key stakeholder goals and objectives?
<--- Score

86. How do you gather requirements?
<--- Score

87. In what way can you redefine the criteria of choice clients have in your category in your favor?
<--- Score

88. What scope do you want your strategy to cover?
<--- Score

89. Is the team adequately staffed with the desired cross-functionality? If not, what additional resources are available to the team?

<--- Score

90. What specifically is the problem? Where does it occur? When does it occur? What is its extent?
<--- Score

91. How will the Applications Infrastructure team and the group measure complete success of Applications Infrastructure?
<--- Score

92. What constraints exist that might impact the team?
<--- Score

93. Who is gathering information?
<--- Score

94. What are the dynamics of the communication plan?
<--- Score

95. Is it clearly defined in and to your organization what you do?
<--- Score

96. If substitutes have been appointed, have they been briefed on the Applications Infrastructure goals and received regular communications as to the progress to date?
<--- Score

97. What scope to assess?
<--- Score

98. How are consistent Applications Infrastructure

definitions important?

<--- Score

99. How did the Applications Infrastructure manager receive input to the development of a Applications Infrastructure improvement plan and the estimated completion dates/times of each activity?

<--- Score

100. Is there a Applications Infrastructure management charter, including stakeholder case, problem and goal statements, scope, milestones, roles and responsibilities, communication plan?

<--- Score

101. How would you define the culture at your organization, how susceptible is it to Applications Infrastructure changes?

<--- Score

102. What sources do you use to gather information for a Applications Infrastructure study?

<--- Score

103. Have all of the relationships been defined properly?

<--- Score

104. Does the team have regular meetings?

<--- Score

105. Is the scope of Applications Infrastructure defined?

<--- Score

106. What are the Roles and Responsibilities for each team member and its leadership? Where is this documented?
<--- Score

107. What is the worst case scenario?
<--- Score

108. Are the Applications Infrastructure requirements complete?
<--- Score

109. Are the Applications Infrastructure requirements testable?
<--- Score

110. How do you manage changes in Applications Infrastructure requirements?
<--- Score

111. What are the boundaries of the scope? What is in bounds and what is not? What is the start point? What is the stop point?
<--- Score

112. What are the record-keeping requirements of Applications Infrastructure activities?
<--- Score

113. Has the improvement team collected the 'voice of the customer' (obtained feedback – qualitative and quantitative)?
<--- Score

114. Has a Applications Infrastructure requirement not been met?

<--- Score

115. What are the requirements for audit information?
<--- Score

116. What key stakeholder process output measure(s) does Applications Infrastructure leverage and how?
<--- Score

117. Is there a clear Applications Infrastructure case definition?
<--- Score

118. What critical content must be communicated – who, what, when, where, and how?
<--- Score

119. Has your scope been defined?
<--- Score

120. Is the Applications Infrastructure scope manageable?
<--- Score

121. What is out-of-scope initially?
<--- Score

122. Are different versions of process maps needed to account for the different types of inputs?
<--- Score

123. Has the direction changed at all during the course of Applications Infrastructure? If so, when did it change and why?
<--- Score

124. What customer feedback methods were used to solicit their input?
<--- Score

125. Is the current 'as is' process being followed? If not, what are the discrepancies?
<--- Score

126. What are the Applications Infrastructure tasks and definitions?
<--- Score

127. Is Applications Infrastructure currently on schedule according to the plan?
<--- Score

128. Do you have a Applications Infrastructure success story or case study ready to tell and share?
<--- Score

129. How do you think the partners involved in Applications Infrastructure would have defined success?
<--- Score

130. What would be the goal or target for a Applications Infrastructure's improvement team?
<--- Score

131. Are resources adequate for the scope?
<--- Score

132. What sort of initial information to gather?
<--- Score

133. How do you manage scope?

<--- Score

134. What are the core elements of the Applications Infrastructure business case?
<--- Score

Add up total points for this section:
_____ = Total points for this section

Divided by: _____ (number of
statements answered) = _____
Average score for this section

Transfer your score to the Applications
Infrastructure Index at the beginning of
the Self-Assessment.

CRITERION #3: MEASURE:

INTENT: Gather the correct data.
Measure the current performance and
evolution of the situation.

In my belief, the answer to this
question is clearly defined:

5 Strongly Agree

4 Agree

3 Neutral

2 Disagree

1 Strongly Disagree

1. Did you tackle the cause or the symptom?
<--- Score

2. How will you measure success?
<--- Score

3. Where can you go to verify the info?
<--- Score

4. When are costs are incurred?
<--- Score

5. Does the Applications Infrastructure task fit the client's priorities?
<--- Score

6. Are there any easy-to-implement alternatives to Applications Infrastructure? Sometimes other solutions are available that do not require the cost implications of a full-blown project?
<--- Score

7. How will effects be measured?
<--- Score

8. What does losing customers cost your organization?
<--- Score

9. How will success or failure be measured?
<--- Score

10. How are you verifying it?
<--- Score

11. How do you verify if Applications Infrastructure is built right?
<--- Score

12. Which Applications Infrastructure impacts are significant?
<--- Score

13. Do you aggressively reward and promote the people who have the biggest impact on creating excellent Applications Infrastructure services/

products?
<--- Score

14. How do you aggregate measures across priorities?
<--- Score

15. What happens if cost savings do not materialize?
<--- Score

16. What is your Applications Infrastructure quality cost segregation study?
<--- Score

17. Where is the cost?
<--- Score

18. How can you reduce costs?
<--- Score

19. What are your key Applications Infrastructure organizational performance measures, including key short and longer-term financial measures?
<--- Score

20. What measurements are possible, practicable and meaningful?
<--- Score

21. What is the root cause(s) of the problem?
<--- Score

22. Are actual costs in line with budgeted costs?
<--- Score

23. Is the cost worth the Applications

Infrastructure effort ?
<--- Score

24. How do you verify your resources?
<--- Score

25. What is the cause of any Applications Infrastructure gaps?
<--- Score

26. Why do the measurements/indicators matter?
<--- Score

27. How are measurements made?
<--- Score

28. What would be a real cause for concern?
<--- Score

29. Are Applications Infrastructure vulnerabilities categorized and prioritized?
<--- Score

30. What do you measure and why?
<--- Score

31. How will you measure your Applications Infrastructure effectiveness?
<--- Score

32. What are the Applications Infrastructure investment costs?
<--- Score

33. What are hidden Applications Infrastructure quality costs?

<--- Score

34. How do you measure lifecycle phases?
<--- Score

35. Among the Applications Infrastructure product and service cost to be estimated, which is considered hardest to estimate?
<--- Score

36. How will measures be used to manage and adapt?
<--- Score

37. Why a Applications Infrastructure focus?
<--- Score

38. What do people want to verify?
<--- Score

39. How do you measure efficient delivery of Applications Infrastructure services?
<--- Score

40. Are you aware of what could cause a problem?
<--- Score

41. Which costs should be taken into account?
<--- Score

42. What could cause delays in the schedule?
<--- Score

43. What drives O&M cost?
<--- Score

44. What are your customers expectations and

measures?

<--- Score

45. How do you measure success?

<--- Score

46. How long to keep data and how to manage retention costs?

<--- Score

47. What are you verifying?

<--- Score

48. Are there competing Applications Infrastructure priorities?

<--- Score

49. How is progress measured?

<--- Score

50. Are the units of measure consistent?

<--- Score

51. How do you control the overall costs of your work processes?

<--- Score

52. Is it possible to estimate the impact of unanticipated complexity such as wrong or failed assumptions, feedback, etcetera on proposed reforms?

<--- Score

53. Have design-to-cost goals been established?

<--- Score

54. What tests verify requirements?
<--- Score

55. How are costs allocated?
<--- Score

56. Why do you expend time and effort to implement measurement, for whom?
<--- Score

57. What does verifying compliance entail?
<--- Score

58. What does your operating model cost?
<--- Score

59. What are the strategic priorities for this year?
<--- Score

60. How can a Applications Infrastructure test verify your ideas or assumptions?
<--- Score

61. How do you verify the authenticity of the data and information used?
<--- Score

62. What are the Applications Infrastructure key cost drivers?
<--- Score

63. Where is it measured?
<--- Score

64. What are the costs of delaying Applications Infrastructure action?

<--- Score

65. Are you able to realize any cost savings?
<--- Score

66. What users will be impacted?
<--- Score

67. What can be used to verify compliance?
<--- Score

68. What is measured? Why?
<--- Score

69. Is the solution cost-effective?
<--- Score

70. What could cause you to change course?
<--- Score

71. What potential environmental factors impact the Applications Infrastructure effort?
<--- Score

72. What methods are feasible and acceptable to estimate the impact of reforms?
<--- Score

73. How do you verify Applications Infrastructure completeness and accuracy?
<--- Score

74. Are there measurements based on task performance?
<--- Score

75. What is the total fixed cost?
<--- Score

76. What are the estimated costs of proposed changes?
<--- Score

77. What evidence is there and what is measured?
<--- Score

78. Was a business case (cost/benefit) developed?
<--- Score

79. What are the current costs of the Applications Infrastructure process?
<--- Score

80. Does a Applications Infrastructure quantification method exist?
<--- Score

81. What relevant entities could be measured?
<--- Score

82. Who should receive measurement reports?
<--- Score

83. Do the benefits outweigh the costs?
<--- Score

84. What measurements are being captured?
<--- Score

85. What is the total cost related to deploying Applications Infrastructure, including any consulting or professional services?

<--- Score

86. What are the types and number of measures to use?
<--- Score

87. How can you measure the performance?
<--- Score

88. What are the costs and benefits?
<--- Score

89. What is an unallowable cost?
<--- Score

90. What details are required of the Applications Infrastructure cost structure?
<--- Score

91. What causes extra work or rework?
<--- Score

92. Are missed Applications Infrastructure opportunities costing your organization money?
<--- Score

93. How will your organization measure success?
<--- Score

94. How can you reduce the costs of obtaining inputs?
<--- Score

95. What are your primary costs, revenues, assets?
<--- Score

96. When a disaster occurs, who gets priority?

<--- Score

97. How sensitive must the Applications Infrastructure strategy be to cost?
<--- Score

98. How much does it cost?
<--- Score

99. What are your operating costs?
<--- Score

100. Do you have any cost Applications Infrastructure limitation requirements?
<--- Score

101. How can you measure Applications Infrastructure in a systematic way?
<--- Score

102. How will costs be allocated?
<--- Score

103. How do you measure variability?
<--- Score

104. At what cost?
<--- Score

105. Are supply costs steady or fluctuating?
<--- Score

106. How do you quantify and qualify impacts?
<--- Score

107. Have you included everything in your

Applications Infrastructure cost models?
<--- Score

108. Are you taking your company in the direction of better and revenue or cheaper and cost?
<--- Score

109. How frequently do you verify your Applications Infrastructure strategy?
<--- Score

110. How do you verify and develop ideas and innovations?
<--- Score

111. Are the measurements objective?
<--- Score

112. How is the value delivered by Applications Infrastructure being measured?
<--- Score

113. What are allowable costs?
<--- Score

114. What causes investor action?
<--- Score

115. How can you manage cost down?
<--- Score

116. Is there an opportunity to verify requirements?
<--- Score

117. How do you verify and validate the Applications Infrastructure data?

<--- Score

118. How is performance measured?
<--- Score

119. Are indirect costs charged to the Applications Infrastructure program?
<--- Score

120. Who is involved in verifying compliance?
<--- Score

121. Do you verify that corrective actions were taken?
<--- Score

122. Which measures and indicators matter?
<--- Score

123. What causes innovation to fail or succeed in your organization?
<--- Score

124. How do you prevent mis-estimating cost?
<--- Score

125. How frequently do you track Applications Infrastructure measures?
<--- Score

126. What does a Test Case verify?
<--- Score

127. What are the costs?
<--- Score

128. Will Applications Infrastructure have an impact

on current business continuity, disaster recovery processes and/or infrastructure?
<--- Score

129. What causes mismanagement?
<--- Score

130. Do you have an issue in getting priority?
<--- Score

Add up total points for this section:
_ _ _ _ _ = Total points for this section

Divided by: _ _ _ _ _ _ (number of statements answered) = _ _ _ _ _ _
Average score for this section

Transfer your score to the Applications Infrastructure Index at the beginning of the Self-Assessment.

CRITERION #4: ANALYZE:

INTENT: Analyze causes, assumptions and hypotheses.

In my belief, the answer to this question is clearly defined:

5 Strongly Agree

4 Agree

3 Neutral

2 Disagree

1 Strongly Disagree

1. What other organizational variables, such as reward systems or communication systems, affect the performance of this Applications Infrastructure process?
<--- Score

2. Is there an established change management process?
<--- Score

3. What is the Applications Infrastructure Driver?
<--- Score

4. What were the crucial 'moments of truth' on the process map?
<--- Score

5. Do your contracts/agreements contain data security obligations?
<--- Score

6. Were Pareto charts (or similar) used to portray the 'heavy hitters' (or key sources of variation)?
<--- Score

7. How do your work systems and key work processes relate to and capitalize on your core competencies?
<--- Score

8. Where can you get qualified talent today?
<--- Score

9. What qualifications do Applications Infrastructure leaders need?
<--- Score

10. How has the Applications Infrastructure data been gathered?
<--- Score

11. Have the problem and goal statements been updated to reflect the additional knowledge gained from the analyze phase?
<--- Score

12. How do you ensure that the Applications Infrastructure opportunity is realistic?
<--- Score

13. What are your outputs?
<--- Score

14. How do you promote understanding that opportunity for improvement is not criticism of the status quo, or the people who created the status quo?
<--- Score

15. Is the suppliers process defined and controlled?
<--- Score

16. What is the Value Stream Mapping?
<--- Score

17. How many input/output points does it require?
<--- Score

18. How is the data gathered?
<--- Score

19. Is the required Applications Infrastructure data gathered?
<--- Score

20. What systems/processes must you excel at?
<--- Score

21. What qualifies as competition?
<--- Score

22. Which Applications Infrastructure data should be retained?

<--- Score

23. How does the organization define, manage, and improve its Applications Infrastructure processes?
<--- Score

24. What is your organizations system for selecting qualified vendors?
<--- Score

25. Are your outputs consistent?
<--- Score

26. What is your organizations process which leads to recognition of value generation?
<--- Score

27. Who qualifies to gain access to data?
<--- Score

28. A compounding model resolution with available relevant data can often provide insight towards a solution methodology; which Applications Infrastructure models, tools and techniques are necessary?
<--- Score

29. How is Applications Infrastructure data gathered?
<--- Score

30. What are the personnel training and qualifications required?
<--- Score

31. Who gets your output?

<--- Score

32. How can risk management be tied procedurally to process elements?
<--- Score

33. Who is involved with workflow mapping?
<--- Score

34. Have any additional benefits been identified that will result from closing all or most of the gaps?
<--- Score

35. Are all staff in core Applications Infrastructure subjects Highly Qualified?
<--- Score

36. What is the oversight process?
<--- Score

37. Was a cause-and-effect diagram used to explore the different types of causes (or sources of variation)?
<--- Score

38. How will corresponding data be collected?
<--- Score

39. How often will data be collected for measures?
<--- Score

40. How will the data be checked for quality?
<--- Score

41. What Applications Infrastructure data should be collected?
<--- Score

42. How do you measure the operational performance of your key work systems and processes, including productivity, cycle time, and other appropriate measures of process effectiveness, efficiency, and innovation?
<--- Score

43. What conclusions were drawn from the team's data collection and analysis? How did the team reach these conclusions?
<--- Score

44. Think about some of the processes you undertake within your organization, which do you own?
<--- Score

45. How was the detailed process map generated, verified, and validated?
<--- Score

46. How difficult is it to qualify what Applications Infrastructure ROI is?
<--- Score

47. Do you understand your management processes today?
<--- Score

48. How do you use Applications Infrastructure data and information to support organizational decision making and innovation?
<--- Score

49. What are the revised rough estimates of the financial savings/opportunity for Applications

Infrastructure improvements?
<--- Score

50. Where is the data coming from to measure compliance?
<--- Score

51. What Applications Infrastructure metrics are outputs of the process?
<--- Score

52. Is the Applications Infrastructure process severely broken such that a re-design is necessary?
<--- Score

53. Should you invest in industry-recognized qualifications?
<--- Score

54. What tools were used to generate the list of possible causes?
<--- Score

55. Can you add value to the current Applications Infrastructure decision-making process (largely qualitative) by incorporating uncertainty modeling (more quantitative)?
<--- Score

56. Do you have the authority to produce the output?
<--- Score

57. What internal processes need improvement?
<--- Score

58. How is data used for program management and

improvement?
<--- Score

59. What output to create?
<--- Score

60. How are outputs preserved and protected?
<--- Score

61. Has an output goal been set?
<--- Score

62. What will drive Applications Infrastructure change?
<--- Score

63. Record-keeping requirements flow from the records needed as inputs, outputs, controls and for transformation of a Applications Infrastructure process, are the records needed as inputs to the Applications Infrastructure process available?
<--- Score

64. What does the data say about the performance of the stakeholder process?
<--- Score

65. What controls do you have in place to protect data?
<--- Score

66. What are your key performance measures or indicators and in-process measures for the control and improvement of your Applications Infrastructure processes?
<--- Score

67. What are your current levels and trends in key measures or indicators of Applications Infrastructure product and process performance that are important to and directly serve your customers? How do these results compare with the performance of your competitors and other organizations with similar offerings?
<--- Score

68. What methods do you use to gather Applications Infrastructure data?
<--- Score

69. Is there any way to speed up the process?
<--- Score

70. What are the disruptive Applications Infrastructure technologies that enable your organization to radically change your business processes?
<--- Score

71. Do staff qualifications match your project?
<--- Score

72. What qualifications and skills do you need?
<--- Score

73. Did any additional data need to be collected?
<--- Score

74. What data do you need to collect?
<--- Score

75. Do your leaders quickly bounce back from

setbacks?
<--- Score

76. What Applications Infrastructure data will be collected?
<--- Score

77. Do quality systems drive continuous improvement?
<--- Score

78. Has data output been validated?
<--- Score

79. Is data and process analysis, root cause analysis and quantifying the gap/opportunity in place?
<--- Score

80. Who is involved in the management review process?
<--- Score

81. How do you define collaboration and team output?
<--- Score

82. How do mission and objectives affect the Applications Infrastructure processes of your organization?
<--- Score

83. What qualifications are needed?
<--- Score

84. Are Applications Infrastructure changes recognized early enough to be approved through

the regular process?
<--- Score

85. Is pre-qualification of suppliers carried out?
<--- Score

86. What qualifications are necessary?
<--- Score

87. How is the way you as the leader think and process information affecting your organizational culture?
<--- Score

88. What Applications Infrastructure data should be managed?
<--- Score

89. What kind of crime could a potential new hire have committed that would not only not disqualify him/her from being hired by your organization, but would actually indicate that he/she might be a particularly good fit?
<--- Score

90. How will the change process be managed?
<--- Score

91. How much data can be collected in the given timeframe?
<--- Score

92. What are evaluation criteria for the output?
<--- Score

93. What are your Applications Infrastructure processes?

<--- Score

94. Who owns what data?
<--- Score

95. What were the financial benefits resulting from
any 'ground fruit or low-hanging fruit' (quick fixes)?
<--- Score

96. How is the Applications Infrastructure Value
Stream Mapping managed?
<--- Score

97. What data is gathered?
<--- Score

98. What tools were used to narrow the list of possible
causes?
<--- Score

99. Are gaps between current performance and the
goal performance identified?
<--- Score

100. What is the output?
<--- Score

101. Do you, as a leader, bounce back quickly from
setbacks?
<--- Score

102. Is the performance gap determined?
<--- Score

103. Is the gap/opportunity displayed and
communicated in financial terms?

<--- Score

104. What quality tools were used to get through the analyze phase?
<--- Score

105. What training and qualifications will you need?
<--- Score

106. What is the complexity of the output produced?
<--- Score

107. Did any value-added analysis or 'lean thinking' take place to identify some of the gaps shown on the 'as is' process map?
<--- Score

108. Are all team members qualified for all tasks?
<--- Score

109. What are your current levels and trends in key Applications Infrastructure measures or indicators of product and process performance that are important to and directly serve your customers?
<--- Score

110. How do you implement and manage your work processes to ensure that they meet design requirements?
<--- Score

111. Were there any improvement opportunities identified from the process analysis?
<--- Score

112. Think about the functions involved in your Applications Infrastructure project, what processes flow from these functions?
<--- Score

113. Are you missing Applications Infrastructure opportunities?
<--- Score

114. What successful thing are you doing today that may be blinding you to new growth opportunities?
<--- Score

115. Have you defined which data is gathered how?
<--- Score

116. What information qualified as important?
<--- Score

117. Do your employees have the opportunity to do what they do best everyday?
<--- Score

118. What is the cost of poor quality as supported by the team's analysis?
<--- Score

119. Where is Applications Infrastructure data gathered?
<--- Score

120. What other jobs or tasks affect the performance of the steps in the Applications Infrastructure process?
<--- Score

121. Is the final output clearly identified?

<--- Score

122. How will the Applications Infrastructure data be captured?
<--- Score

123. What process should you select for improvement?
<--- Score

124. What are the Applications Infrastructure business drivers?
<--- Score

125. Was a detailed process map created to amplify critical steps of the 'as is' stakeholder process?
<--- Score

126. What, related to, Applications Infrastructure processes does your organization outsource?
<--- Score

127. What do you need to qualify?
<--- Score

128. What Applications Infrastructure data do you gather or use now?
<--- Score

129. What are the best opportunities for value improvement?
<--- Score

130. What did the team gain from developing a sub-process map?
<--- Score

131. Were any designed experiments used to generate additional insight into the data analysis?
<--- Score

Add up total points for this section:
_____ = Total points for this section

Divided by: _____ (number of statements answered) = _____
Average score for this section

Transfer your score to the Applications Infrastructure Index at the beginning of the Self-Assessment.

CRITERION #5: IMPROVE:

INTENT: Develop a practical solution.
Innovate, establish and test the
solution and to measure the results.

In my belief, the answer to this
question is clearly defined:

5 Strongly Agree

4 Agree

3 Neutral

2 Disagree

1 Strongly Disagree

1. What are your current levels and trends in key
measures or indicators of workforce and leader
development?
<--- Score

2. Who will be responsible for documenting the
Applications Infrastructure requirements in detail?
<--- Score

3. Who are the key stakeholders for the Applications Infrastructure evaluation?
<--- Score

4. Was a Applications Infrastructure charter developed?
<--- Score

5. What should a proof of concept or pilot accomplish?
<--- Score

6. Do you need to do a usability evaluation?
<--- Score

7. What lessons, if any, from a pilot were incorporated into the design of the full-scale solution?
<--- Score

8. What can you do to improve?
<--- Score

9. Who controls the risk?
<--- Score

10. What Applications Infrastructure improvements can be made?
<--- Score

11. How do the Applications Infrastructure results compare with the performance of your competitors and other organizations with similar offerings?
<--- Score

12. How significant is the improvement in the eyes of the end user?

<--- Score

13. Is the measure of success for Applications Infrastructure understandable to a variety of people?
<--- Score

14. How do you measure progress and evaluate training effectiveness?
<--- Score

15. Explorations of the frontiers of Applications Infrastructure will help you build influence, improve Applications Infrastructure, optimize decision making, and sustain change, what is your approach?
<--- Score

16. How do you improve productivity?
<--- Score

17. How will you know that you have improved?
<--- Score

18. Do you combine technical expertise with business knowledge and Applications Infrastructure Key topics include lifecycles, development approaches, requirements and how to make a business case?
<--- Score

19. In the past few months, what is the smallest change you have made that has had the biggest positive result? What was it about that small change that produced the large return?
<--- Score

20. What needs improvement? Why?
<--- Score

21. How will you know that a change is an improvement?
<--- Score

22. How do you improve your likelihood of success ?
<--- Score

23. Is Applications Infrastructure documentation maintained?
<--- Score

24. What error proofing will be done to address some of the discrepancies observed in the 'as is' process?
<--- Score

25. Who controls key decisions that will be made?
<--- Score

26. What risks do you need to manage?
<--- Score

27. Are risk management tasks balanced centrally and locally?
<--- Score

28. Risk events: what are the things that could go wrong?
<--- Score

29. How does your organization evaluate strategic Applications Infrastructure success?
<--- Score

30. Do vendor agreements bring new compliance risk ?

<--- Score

31. Applications Infrastructure risk decisions: whose call Is It?
<--- Score

32. How do you go about comparing Applications Infrastructure approaches/solutions?
<--- Score

33. Who will be using the results of the measurement activities?
<--- Score

34. Have you achieved Applications Infrastructure improvements?
<--- Score

35. Who manages supplier risk management in your organization?
<--- Score

36. How does the team improve its work?
<--- Score

37. Are decisions made in a timely manner?
<--- Score

38. Which of the recognised risks out of all risks can be most likely transferred?
<--- Score

39. Why improve in the first place?
<--- Score

40. What alternative responses are available to

manage risk?
<--- Score

41. How do you define the solutions' scope?
<--- Score

42. What tools were used to tap into the creativity and encourage 'outside the box' thinking?
<--- Score

43. Would you develop a Applications Infrastructure Communication Strategy?
<--- Score

44. Can you identify any significant risks or exposures to Applications Infrastructure third- parties (vendors, service providers, alliance partners etc) that concern you?
<--- Score

45. What is the team's contingency plan for potential problems occurring in implementation?
<--- Score

46. Where do you need Applications Infrastructure improvement?
<--- Score

47. What is Applications Infrastructure risk?
<--- Score

48. What tools were most useful during the improve phase?
<--- Score

49. How do you measure improved Applications

Infrastructure service perception, and satisfaction?
<--- Score

50. How do you manage and improve your Applications Infrastructure work systems to deliver customer value and achieve organizational success and sustainability?
<--- Score

51. For estimation problems, how do you develop an estimation statement?
<--- Score

52. What is the risk?
<--- Score

53. Risk factors: what are the characteristics of Applications Infrastructure that make it risky?
<--- Score

54. What resources are required for the improvement efforts?
<--- Score

55. Who makes the Applications Infrastructure decisions in your organization?
<--- Score

56. What strategies for Applications Infrastructure improvement are successful?
<--- Score

57. What assumptions are made about the solution and approach?
<--- Score

58. Is risk periodically assessed?
<--- Score

59. Is any Applications Infrastructure documentation required?
<--- Score

60. What does the 'should be' process map/design look like?
<--- Score

61. How do you keep improving Applications Infrastructure?
<--- Score

62. Are the risks fully understood, reasonable and manageable?
<--- Score

63. How scalable is your Applications Infrastructure solution?
<--- Score

64. How can skill-level changes improve Applications Infrastructure?
<--- Score

65. Are the most efficient solutions problem-specific?
<--- Score

66. Is supporting Applications Infrastructure documentation required?
<--- Score

67. What practices helps your organization to develop its capacity to recognize patterns?

<--- Score

68. How do you improve Applications Infrastructure service perception, and satisfaction?
<--- Score

69. Where do the Applications Infrastructure decisions reside?
<--- Score

70. How do you manage Applications Infrastructure risk?
<--- Score

71. Who are the people involved in developing and implementing Applications Infrastructure?
<--- Score

72. What is the implementation plan?
<--- Score

73. How risky is your organization?
<--- Score

74. Who do you report Applications Infrastructure results to?
<--- Score

75. What were the criteria for evaluating a Applications Infrastructure pilot?
<--- Score

76. Are procedures documented for managing Applications Infrastructure risks?
<--- Score

77. What are the concrete Applications Infrastructure results?
<--- Score

78. Who are the Applications Infrastructure decision makers?
<--- Score

79. Is the Applications Infrastructure documentation thorough?
<--- Score

80. Have you identified breakpoints and/or risk tolerances that will trigger broad consideration of a potential need for intervention or modification of strategy?
<--- Score

81. Are events managed to resolution?
<--- Score

82. How can you better manage risk?
<--- Score

83. Is the Applications Infrastructure risk managed?
<--- Score

84. How will you measure the results?
<--- Score

85. What current systems have to be understood and/or changed?
<--- Score

86. What tools were used to evaluate the potential

solutions?

<--- Score

87. Are risk triggers captured?

<--- Score

88. At what point will vulnerability assessments be performed once Applications Infrastructure is put into production (e.g., ongoing Risk Management after implementation)?

<--- Score

89. What were the underlying assumptions on the cost-benefit analysis?

<--- Score

90. What is Applications Infrastructure's impact on utilizing the best solution(s)?

<--- Score

91. To what extent does management recognize Applications Infrastructure as a tool to increase the results?

<--- Score

92. How can the phases of Applications Infrastructure development be identified?

<--- Score

93. Is the Applications Infrastructure solution sustainable?

<--- Score

94. What attendant changes will need to be made to ensure that the solution is successful?

<--- Score

95. What tools do you use once you have decided on a Applications Infrastructure strategy and more importantly how do you choose?
<--- Score

96. What is the Applications Infrastructure's sustainability risk?
<--- Score

97. For decision problems, how do you develop a decision statement?
<--- Score

98. How will you recognize and celebrate results?
<--- Score

99. Does the goal represent a desired result that can be measured?
<--- Score

100. How can you improve Applications Infrastructure?
<--- Score

101. What do you want to improve?
<--- Score

102. How are policy decisions made and where?
<--- Score

103. What actually has to improve and by how much?
<--- Score

104. What to do with the results or outcomes of measurements?

<--- Score

105. Risk Identification: What are the possible risk events your organization faces in relation to Applications Infrastructure?
<--- Score

106. What criteria will you use to assess your Applications Infrastructure risks?
<--- Score

107. Which Applications Infrastructure solution is appropriate?
<--- Score

108. How can you improve performance?
<--- Score

109. What area needs the greatest improvement?
<--- Score

110. What communications are necessary to support the implementation of the solution?
<--- Score

111. Do you have the optimal project management team structure?
<--- Score

112. Do you cover the five essential competencies: Communication, Collaboration,Innovation, Adaptability, and Leadership that improve an organizations ability to leverage the new Applications Infrastructure in a volatile global economy?
<--- Score

113. Is there a high likelihood that any recommendations will achieve their intended results?
<--- Score

114. What went well, what should change, what can improve?
<--- Score

115. What are the implications of the one critical Applications Infrastructure decision 10 minutes, 10 months, and 10 years from now?
<--- Score

116. Is there any other Applications Infrastructure solution?
<--- Score

117. What are the affordable Applications Infrastructure risks?
<--- Score

118. Are you assessing Applications Infrastructure and risk?
<--- Score

119. Does a good decision guarantee a good outcome?
<--- Score

120. What is the magnitude of the improvements?
<--- Score

121. How do you measure risk?
<--- Score

122. How will you know when its improved?
<--- Score

123. Who manages Applications Infrastructure risk?
<--- Score

124. Is the scope clearly documented?
<--- Score

125. How do you decide how much to remunerate an employee?
<--- Score

126. How do you link measurement and risk?
<--- Score

127. If you could go back in time five years, what decision would you make differently? What is your best guess as to what decision you're making today you might regret five years from now?
<--- Score

128. How are Applications Infrastructure risks managed?
<--- Score

129. Will the controls trigger any other risks?
<--- Score

130. Who will be responsible for making the decisions to include or exclude requested changes once Applications Infrastructure is underway?
<--- Score

131. Can the solution be designed and implemented within an acceptable time period?

<--- Score

132. What are the expected Applications
Infrastructure results?
<--- Score

133. When you map the key players in your own work
and the types/domains of relationships with them,
which relationships do you find easy and which
challenging, and why?
<--- Score

Add up total points for this section:
_____ = Total points for this section

Divided by: _____ (number of
statements answered) = _____
Average score for this section

Transfer your score to the Applications
Infrastructure Index at the beginning of
the Self-Assessment.

CRITERION #6: CONTROL:

INTENT: Implement the practical solution. Maintain the performance and correct possible complications.

In my belief, the answer to this question is clearly defined:

5 Strongly Agree

4 Agree

3 Neutral

2 Disagree

1 Strongly Disagree

1. Do the viable solutions scale to future needs?
<--- Score

2. What are the known security controls?
<--- Score

3. Do you monitor the Applications Infrastructure decisions made and fine tune them as they evolve?
<--- Score

4. Are suggested corrective/restorative actions indicated on the response plan for known causes to problems that might surface?
<--- Score

5. What is the control/monitoring plan?
<--- Score

6. Are operating procedures consistent?
<--- Score

7. Is there a Applications Infrastructure Communication plan covering who needs to get what information when?
<--- Score

8. Are there documented procedures?
<--- Score

9. Who will be in control?
<--- Score

10. How do you establish and deploy modified action plans if circumstances require a shift in plans and rapid execution of new plans?
<--- Score

11. In the case of a Applications Infrastructure project, the criteria for the audit derive from implementation objectives, an audit of a Applications Infrastructure project involves assessing whether the recommendations outlined for implementation have been met, can you track that any Applications Infrastructure project is implemented as planned, and is it working?

<--- Score

12. What is your theory of human motivation, and how does your compensation plan fit with that view?
<--- Score

13. How do senior leaders actions reflect a commitment to the organizations Applications Infrastructure values?
<--- Score

14. How will new or emerging customer needs/requirements be checked/communicated to orient the process toward meeting the new specifications and continually reducing variation?
<--- Score

15. What are the key elements of your Applications Infrastructure performance improvement system, including your evaluation, organizational learning, and innovation processes?
<--- Score

16. Who has control over resources?
<--- Score

17. How do you spread information?
<--- Score

18. What other areas of the group might benefit from the Applications Infrastructure team's improvements, knowledge, and learning?
<--- Score

19. How do you select, collect, align, and integrate Applications Infrastructure data and information for

tracking daily operations and overall organizational performance, including progress relative to strategic objectives and action plans?
<--- Score

20. How is Applications Infrastructure project cost planned, managed, monitored?
<--- Score

21. How do you plan for the cost of succession?
<--- Score

22. What adjustments to the strategies are needed?
<--- Score

23. What Applications Infrastructure standards are applicable?
<--- Score

24. Where do ideas that reach policy makers and planners as proposals for Applications Infrastructure strengthening and reform actually originate?
<--- Score

25. Are you measuring, monitoring and predicting Applications Infrastructure activities to optimize operations and profitability, and enhancing outcomes?
<--- Score

26. Are the Applications Infrastructure standards challenging?
<--- Score

27. Does the Applications Infrastructure performance meet the customer's requirements?

<--- Score

28. What do you measure to verify effectiveness gains?
<--- Score

29. Will the team be available to assist members in planning investigations?
<--- Score

30. Can you adapt and adjust to changing Applications Infrastructure situations?
<--- Score

31. Is reporting being used or needed?
<--- Score

32. Have new or revised work instructions resulted?
<--- Score

33. Are the planned controls working?
<--- Score

34. How will the process owner and team be able to hold the gains?
<--- Score

35. What key inputs and outputs are being measured on an ongoing basis?
<--- Score

36. Is there documentation that will support the successful operation of the improvement?
<--- Score

37. Are the planned controls in place?

<--- Score

38. What do you stand for--and what are you against?
<--- Score

39. Will your goals reflect your program budget?
<--- Score

40. Who controls critical resources?
<--- Score

41. How might the group capture best practices and lessons learned so as to leverage improvements?
<--- Score

42. What are you attempting to measure/monitor?
<--- Score

43. Are pertinent alerts monitored, analyzed and distributed to appropriate personnel?
<--- Score

44. How widespread is its use?
<--- Score

45. What do your reports reflect?
<--- Score

46. How do controls support value?
<--- Score

47. How will the process owner verify improvement in present and future sigma levels, process capabilities?
<--- Score

48. How will input, process, and output variables be checked to detect for sub-optimal conditions?
<--- Score

49. What are customers monitoring?
<--- Score

50. What are the performance and scale of the Applications Infrastructure tools?
<--- Score

51. How can you best use all of your knowledge repositories to enhance learning and sharing?
<--- Score

52. What is the recommended frequency of auditing?
<--- Score

53. Will existing staff require re-training, for example, to learn new business processes?
<--- Score

54. Will any special training be provided for results interpretation?
<--- Score

55. What should the next improvement project be that is related to Applications Infrastructure?
<--- Score

56. Is there a control plan in place for sustaining improvements (short and long-term)?
<--- Score

57. How will Applications Infrastructure decisions be made and monitored?

<--- Score

58. Against what alternative is success being measured?
<--- Score

59. Is there a recommended audit plan for routine surveillance inspections of Applications Infrastructure's gains?
<--- Score

60. What quality tools were useful in the control phase?
<--- Score

61. Is a response plan established and deployed?
<--- Score

62. How will report readings be checked to effectively monitor performance?
<--- Score

63. What can you control?
<--- Score

64. Does job training on the documented procedures need to be part of the process team's education and training?
<--- Score

65. Is a response plan in place for when the input, process, or output measures indicate an 'out-of-control' condition?
<--- Score

66. What are your results for key measures or

indicators of the accomplishment of your Applications Infrastructure strategy and action plans, including building and strengthening core competencies?
<--- Score

67. Are documented procedures clear and easy to follow for the operators?
<--- Score

68. Who sets the Applications Infrastructure standards?
<--- Score

69. How likely is the current Applications Infrastructure plan to come in on schedule or on budget?
<--- Score

70. How do your controls stack up?
<--- Score

71. Can support from partners be adjusted?
<--- Score

72. How do you encourage people to take control and responsibility?
<--- Score

73. Who is the Applications Infrastructure process owner?
<--- Score

74. Do you monitor the effectiveness of your Applications Infrastructure activities?
<--- Score

75. Implementation Planning: is a pilot needed to test the changes before a full roll out occurs?
<--- Score

76. How will the day-to-day responsibilities for monitoring and continual improvement be transferred from the improvement team to the process owner?
<--- Score

77. Does Applications Infrastructure appropriately measure and monitor risk?
<--- Score

78. Do the Applications Infrastructure decisions you make today help people and the planet tomorrow?
<--- Score

79. What are the critical parameters to watch?
<--- Score

80. Is knowledge gained on process shared and institutionalized?
<--- Score

81. Are controls in place and consistently applied?
<--- Score

82. Is the Applications Infrastructure test/monitoring cost justified?
<--- Score

83. How do you monitor usage and cost?
<--- Score

84. Is there a standardized process?

<--- Score

85. How will you measure your QA plan's effectiveness?
<--- Score

86. Is there a documented and implemented monitoring plan?
<--- Score

87. Who is going to spread your message?
<--- Score

88. Has the Applications Infrastructure value of standards been quantified?
<--- Score

89. Is there a transfer of ownership and knowledge to process owner and process team tasked with the responsibilities.
<--- Score

90. How is change control managed?
<--- Score

91. Are new process steps, standards, and documentation ingrained into normal operations?
<--- Score

92. What other systems, operations, processes, and infrastructures (hiring practices, staffing, training, incentives/rewards, metrics/dashboards/scorecards, etc.) need updates, additions, changes, or deletions in order to facilitate knowledge transfer and improvements?
<--- Score

93. Has the improved process and its steps been standardized?
<--- Score

94. How do you plan on providing proper recognition and disclosure of supporting companies?
<--- Score

95. What is the standard for acceptable Applications Infrastructure performance?
<--- Score

96. You may have created your quality measures at a time when you lacked resources, technology wasn't up to the required standard, or low service levels were the industry norm. Have those circumstances changed?
<--- Score

97. Is new knowledge gained imbedded in the response plan?
<--- Score

98. Does a troubleshooting guide exist or is it needed?
<--- Score

99. Does the response plan contain a definite closed loop continual improvement scheme (e.g., plan-do-check-act)?
<--- Score

100. Act/Adjust: What Do you Need to Do Differently?
<--- Score

101. Is there an action plan in case of emergencies?

<--- Score

Add up total points for this section:
_____ = Total points for this section

Divided by: _____ (number of
statements answered) = _____
Average score for this section

Transfer your score to the Applications
Infrastructure Index at the beginning of
the Self-Assessment.

CRITERION #7: SUSTAIN:

INTENT: Retain the benefits.

In my belief, the answer to this question is clearly defined:

5 Strongly Agree

4 Agree

3 Neutral

2 Disagree

1 Strongly Disagree

1. What have you done to protect your business from competitive encroachment?
<--- Score

2. Why will customers want to buy your organizations products/services?
<--- Score

3. How will you insure seamless interoperability of Applications Infrastructure moving forward?
<--- Score

4. Is there any existing Applications Infrastructure governance structure?
<--- Score

5. What trouble can you get into?
<--- Score

6. Who are four people whose careers you have enhanced?
<--- Score

7. What may be the consequences for the performance of an organization if all stakeholders are not consulted regarding Applications Infrastructure?
<--- Score

8. What is your formula for success in Applications Infrastructure ?
<--- Score

9. Do you feel that more should be done in the Applications Infrastructure area?
<--- Score

10. What unique value proposition (UVP) do you offer?
<--- Score

11. Is the Applications Infrastructure organization completing tasks effectively and efficiently?
<--- Score

12. What is your BATNA (best alternative to a negotiated agreement)?
<--- Score

13. What are the success criteria that will indicate that Applications Infrastructure objectives have been met and the benefits delivered?

<--- Score

14. How do you listen to customers to obtain actionable information?

<--- Score

15. How can you negotiate Applications Infrastructure successfully with a stubborn boss, an irate client, or a deceitful coworker?

<--- Score

16. What are the challenges?

<--- Score

17. What happens if you do not have enough funding?

<--- Score

18. How do you transition from the baseline to the target?

<--- Score

19. What is something you believe that nearly no one agrees with you on?

<--- Score

20. How do you proactively clarify deliverables and Applications Infrastructure quality expectations?

<--- Score

21. Whose voice (department, ethnic group, women, older workers, etc) might you have missed

hearing from in your company, and how might you amplify this voice to create positive momentum for your business?
<--- Score

22. Do you have enough freaky customers in your portfolio pushing you to the limit day in and day out?
<--- Score

23. What are you trying to prove to yourself, and how might it be hijacking your life and business success?
<--- Score

24. What are the barriers to increased Applications Infrastructure production?
<--- Score

25. Are you satisfied with your current role? If not, what is missing from it?
<--- Score

26. What is effective Applications Infrastructure?
<--- Score

27. Are you paying enough attention to the partners your company depends on to succeed?
<--- Score

28. How can you incorporate support to ensure safe and effective use of Applications Infrastructure into the services that you provide?
<--- Score

29. Are the assumptions believable and achievable?
<--- Score

30. At what moment would you think; Will I get fired?
<--- Score

31. What management system can you use to leverage the Applications Infrastructure experience, ideas, and concerns of the people closest to the work to be done?
<--- Score

32. Will there be any necessary staff changes (redundancies or new hires)?
<--- Score

33. If you weren't already in this business, would you enter it today? And if not, what are you going to do about it?
<--- Score

34. Who are your customers?
<--- Score

35. Do you think Applications Infrastructure accomplishes the goals you expect it to accomplish?
<--- Score

36. How long will it take to change?
<--- Score

37. How do you manage Applications Infrastructure Knowledge Management (KM)?
<--- Score

38. Who do you want your customers to become?
<--- Score

39. What is an unauthorized commitment?

<--- Score

40. Instead of going to current contacts for new ideas, what if you reconnected with dormant contacts-- the people you used to know? If you were going reactivate a dormant tie, who would it be?
<--- Score

41. What counts that you are not counting?
<--- Score

42. Who is the main stakeholder, with ultimate responsibility for driving Applications Infrastructure forward?
<--- Score

43. Will it be accepted by users?
<--- Score

44. What happens at your organization when people fail?
<--- Score

45. What are internal and external Applications Infrastructure relations?
<--- Score

46. Why should people listen to you?
<--- Score

47. What potential megatrends could make your business model obsolete?
<--- Score

48. If you do not follow, then how to lead?
<--- Score

49. What are the long-term Applications Infrastructure goals?
<--- Score

50. Is there any reason to believe the opposite of my current belief?
<--- Score

51. Who will provide the final approval of Applications Infrastructure deliverables?
<--- Score

52. What are your personal philosophies regarding Applications Infrastructure and how do they influence your work?
<--- Score

53. Do you have the right capabilities and capacities?
<--- Score

54. What is the overall business strategy?
<--- Score

55. What is the purpose of Applications Infrastructure in relation to the mission?
<--- Score

56. What is your question? Why?
<--- Score

57. What must you excel at?
<--- Score

58. Are all key stakeholders present at all Structured Walkthroughs?

<--- Score

59. What knowledge, skills and characteristics mark a good Applications Infrastructure project manager?
<--- Score

60. What new services of functionality will be implemented next with Applications Infrastructure ?
<--- Score

61. Can you maintain your growth without detracting from the factors that have contributed to your success?
<--- Score

62. How do you make it meaningful in connecting Applications Infrastructure with what users do day-to-day?
<--- Score

63. How do you set Applications Infrastructure stretch targets and how do you get people to not only participate in setting these stretch targets but also that they strive to achieve these?
<--- Score

64. Who else should you help?
<--- Score

65. Why is Applications Infrastructure important for you now?
<--- Score

66. How do you maintain Applications Infrastructure's Integrity?

<--- Score

67. Ask yourself: how would you do this work if you only had one staff member to do it?
<--- Score

68. Is your strategy driving your strategy? Or is the way in which you allocate resources driving your strategy?
<--- Score

69. What did you miss in the interview for the worst hire you ever made?
<--- Score

70. Do you have a flow diagram of what happens?
<--- Score

71. What threat is Applications Infrastructure addressing?
<--- Score

72. Which functions and people interact with the supplier and or customer?
<--- Score

73. What is the funding source for this project?
<--- Score

74. Think of your Applications Infrastructure project, what are the main functions?
<--- Score

75. In the past year, what have you done (or could you have done) to increase the accurate perception of your company/brand as ethical and honest?

<--- Score

76. What are strategies for increasing support and reducing opposition?
<--- Score

77. What will be the consequences to the stakeholder (financial, reputation etc) if Applications Infrastructure does not go ahead or fails to deliver the objectives?
<--- Score

78. How can you become the company that would put you out of business?
<--- Score

79. If your customer were your grandmother, would you tell her to buy what you're selling?
<--- Score

80. In a project to restructure Applications Infrastructure outcomes, which stakeholders would you involve?
<--- Score

81. What are the short and long-term Applications Infrastructure goals?
<--- Score

82. How will you know that the Applications Infrastructure project has been successful?
<--- Score

83. Is it economical; do you have the time and money?
<--- Score

84. How do you govern and fulfill your societal

responsibilities?
<--- Score

85. What is the recommended frequency of auditing?
<--- Score

86. What is the source of the strategies for Applications Infrastructure strengthening and reform?
<--- Score

87. Are you making progress, and are you making progress as Applications Infrastructure leaders?
<--- Score

88. How can you become more high-tech but still be high touch?
<--- Score

89. If no one would ever find out about your accomplishments, how would you lead differently?
<--- Score

90. What is your competitive advantage?
<--- Score

91. Would you rather sell to knowledgeable and informed customers or to uninformed customers?
<--- Score

92. What projects are going on in the organization today, and what resources are those projects using from the resource pools?
<--- Score

93. What have been your experiences in defining long

range Applications Infrastructure goals?
<--- Score

94. What are specific Applications Infrastructure rules to follow?
<--- Score

95. Which individuals, teams or departments will be involved in Applications Infrastructure?
<--- Score

96. How do senior leaders deploy your organizations vision and values through your leadership system, to the workforce, to key suppliers and partners, and to customers and other stakeholders, as appropriate?
<--- Score

97. Are assumptions made in Applications Infrastructure stated explicitly?
<--- Score

98. How are you doing compared to your industry?
<--- Score

99. What are the gaps in your knowledge and experience?
<--- Score

100. How do you determine the key elements that affect Applications Infrastructure workforce satisfaction, how are these elements determined for different workforce groups and segments?
<--- Score

101. What is the overall talent health of your

organization as a whole at senior levels, and for each organization reporting to a member of the Senior Leadership Team?

<--- Score

102. Which Applications Infrastructure goals are the most important?

<--- Score

103. Who is responsible for Applications Infrastructure?

<--- Score

104. What are the usability implications of Applications Infrastructure actions?

<--- Score

105. How do you foster innovation?

<--- Score

106. Is Applications Infrastructure dependent on the successful delivery of a current project?

<--- Score

107. Whom among your colleagues do you trust, and for what?

<--- Score

108. What stupid rule would you most like to kill?

<--- Score

109. What are the business goals Applications Infrastructure is aiming to achieve?

<--- Score

110. What are you challenging?

<--- Score

111. How do you create buy-in?
<--- Score

112. How do you go about securing Applications Infrastructure?
<--- Score

113. Who are the key stakeholders?
<--- Score

114. If you had to leave your organization for a year and the only communication you could have with employees/colleagues was a single paragraph, what would you write?
<--- Score

115. Can the schedule be done in the given time?
<--- Score

116. Why is it important to have senior management support for a Applications Infrastructure project?
<--- Score

117. Do you know what you are doing? And who do you call if you don't?
<--- Score

118. If there were zero limitations, what would you do differently?
<--- Score

119. What are your most important goals for the strategic Applications Infrastructure objectives?
<--- Score

120. Political -is anyone trying to undermine this project?

<--- Score

121. Who is responsible for errors?

<--- Score

122. If you got fired and a new hire took your place, what would she do different?

<--- Score

123. What are current Applications Infrastructure paradigms?

<--- Score

124. How do you assess the Applications Infrastructure pitfalls that are inherent in implementing it?

<--- Score

125. Why not do Applications Infrastructure?

<--- Score

126. How do you engage the workforce, in addition to satisfying them?

<--- Score

127. Do you have past Applications Infrastructure successes?

<--- Score

128. Where can you break convention?

<--- Score

129. How do you accomplish your long range

Applications Infrastructure goals?
<--- Score

130. Who uses your product in ways you never expected?
<--- Score

131. How do you provide a safe environment -physically and emotionally?
<--- Score

132. Do you say no to customers for no reason?
<--- Score

133. Can you do all this work?
<--- Score

134. What business benefits will Applications Infrastructure goals deliver if achieved?
<--- Score

135. What information is critical to your organization that your executives are ignoring?
<--- Score

136. If you had to rebuild your organization without any traditional competitive advantages (i.e., no killer technology, promising research, innovative product/service delivery model, etcetera), how would your people have to approach their work and collaborate together in order to create the necessary conditions for success?
<--- Score

137. How do you foster the skills, knowledge, talents,

attributes, and characteristics you want to have?
<--- Score

138. How do customers see your organization?
<--- Score

139. What are the essentials of internal Applications Infrastructure management?
<--- Score

140. What are the rules and assumptions your industry operates under? What if the opposite were true?
<--- Score

141. What is the craziest thing you can do?
<--- Score

142. How will you ensure you get what you expected?
<--- Score

143. How much contingency will be available in the budget?
<--- Score

144. Is your basic point _____ or _____?
<--- Score

145. What Applications Infrastructure modifications can you make work for you?
<--- Score

146. Which models, tools and techniques are necessary?
<--- Score

147. What is a feasible sequencing of reform initiatives over time?
<--- Score

148. Do you have an implicit bias for capital investments over people investments?
<--- Score

149. Who is on the team?
<--- Score

150. Who is responsible for ensuring appropriate resources (time, people and money) are allocated to Applications Infrastructure?
<--- Score

151. What should you stop doing?
<--- Score

152. If you were responsible for initiating and implementing major changes in your organization, what steps might you take to ensure acceptance of those changes?
<--- Score

153. Is a Applications Infrastructure team work effort in place?
<--- Score

154. What Applications Infrastructure skills are most important?
<--- Score

155. What are the top 3 things at the forefront of your Applications Infrastructure agendas for the next 3 years?

<--- Score

156. Who have you, as a company, historically been when you've been at your best?
<--- Score

157. Is maximizing Applications Infrastructure protection the same as minimizing Applications Infrastructure loss?
<--- Score

158. What would you recommend your friend do if he/she were facing this dilemma?
<--- Score

159. How likely is it that a customer would recommend your company to a friend or colleague?
<--- Score

160. Who do you think the world wants your organization to be?
<--- Score

161. How important is Applications Infrastructure to the user organizations mission?
<--- Score

162. What is your Applications Infrastructure strategy?
<--- Score

163. How is implementation research currently incorporated into each of your goals?
<--- Score

164. What are the potential basics of Applications

Infrastructure fraud?

<--- Score

165. In retrospect, of the projects that you pulled the plug on, what percent do you wish had been allowed to keep going, and what percent do you wish had ended earlier?

<--- Score

166. What are the key enablers to make this Applications Infrastructure move?

<--- Score

167. Who do we want your customers to become?

<--- Score

168. What would have to be true for the option on the table to be the best possible choice?

<--- Score

169. Is Applications Infrastructure realistic, or are you setting yourself up for failure?

<--- Score

170. Do Applications Infrastructure rules make a reasonable demand on a users capabilities?

<--- Score

171. How do you lead with Applications Infrastructure in mind?

<--- Score

172. How do you ensure that implementations of Applications Infrastructure products are done in a way that ensures safety?

<--- Score

173. What is the range of capabilities?
<--- Score

174. What role does communication play in the success or failure of a Applications Infrastructure project?
<--- Score

175. Are you / should you be revolutionary or evolutionary?
<--- Score

176. Do you see more potential in people than they do in themselves?
<--- Score

177. Marketing budgets are tighter, consumers are more skeptical, and social media has changed forever the way we talk about Applications Infrastructure, how do you gain traction?
<--- Score

178. When information truly is ubiquitous, when reach and connectivity are completely global, when computing resources are infinite, and when a whole new set of impossibilities are not only possible, but happening, what will that do to your business?
<--- Score

179. If you find that you havent accomplished one of the goals for one of the steps of the Applications Infrastructure strategy, what will you do to fix it?
<--- Score

180. Who, on the executive team or the board, has

spoken to a customer recently?
<--- Score

181. To whom do you add value?
<--- Score

182. What goals did you miss?
<--- Score

183. How will you motivate the stakeholders with the least vested interest?
<--- Score

184. Who will be responsible for deciding whether Applications Infrastructure goes ahead or not after the initial investigations?
<--- Score

185. Do you have the right people on the bus?
<--- Score

186. What does your signature ensure?
<--- Score

187. Did your employees make progress today?
<--- Score

188. Who will determine interim and final deadlines?
<--- Score

189. How do you track customer value, profitability or financial return, organizational success, and sustainability?
<--- Score

190. Do you think you know, or do you know you

know ?
<--- Score

191. Are you maintaining a past–present–
future perspective throughout the Applications
Infrastructure discussion?
<--- Score

Add up total points for this section:
_____ = Total points for this section

Divided by: _____ (number of
statements answered) = _____
Average score for this section

Transfer your score to the Applications
Infrastructure Index at the beginning of
the Self-Assessment.

Applications Infrastructure and Managing Projects, Criteria for Project Managers:

1.0 Initiating Process Group: Applications Infrastructure

1. Have requirements been tested, approved, and fulfill the Applications Infrastructure project scope?

2. What communication items need improvement?

3. Were sponsors and decision makers available when needed outside regularly scheduled meetings?

4. Do you know the roles & responsibilities required for this Applications Infrastructure project?

5. Did you use a contractor or vendor?

6. How will it affect me?

7. How do you help others satisfy needs?

8. What do they need to know about the Applications Infrastructure project?

9. How well did the chosen processes fit the needs of the Applications Infrastructure project?

10. How will you know you did it?

11. Which of six sigmas dmaic phases focuses on the measurement of internal process that affect factors that are critical to quality?

12. What are the required resources?

13. Will the Applications Infrastructure project meet

the client requirements, and will it achieve the business success criteria that justified doing the Applications Infrastructure project in the first place?

14. Are the changes in your Applications Infrastructure project being formally requested, analyzed, and approved by the appropriate decision makers?

15. What will you do to minimize the impact should a risk event occur?

16. Have you evaluated the teams performance and asked for feedback?

17. What were things that you need to improve?

18. When will the Applications Infrastructure project be done?

19. What will be the pressing issues of tomorrow?

20. What were things that you did well, and could improve, and how?

1.1 Project Charter: Applications Infrastructure

21. Where and how does the team fit within your organization structure?

22. Applications Infrastructure project objective statement: what must the Applications Infrastructure project do?

23. Why use a Applications Infrastructure project charter?

24. What ideas do you have for initial tests of change (PDSA cycles)?

25. Why Outsource?

26. When is a charter needed?

27. Assumptions: what factors, for planning purposes, are you considering to be true?

28. Environmental stewardship and sustainability considerations: what is the process that will be used to ensure compliance with the environmental stewardship policy?

29. How much?

30. How are Applications Infrastructure projects different from operations?

31. Why have you chosen the aim you have set forth?

32. Customer: who are you doing the Applications Infrastructure project for?

33. Review the general mission What system will be affected by the improvement efforts?

34. Who are the stakeholders?

35. If finished, on what date did it finish?

36. What barriers do you predict to your success?

37. Are there special technology requirements?

38. How will you know a change is an improvement?

39. Who ise input and support will this Applications Infrastructure project require?

40. Why do you need to manage scope?

1.2 Stakeholder Register: Applications Infrastructure

41. How much influence do they have on the Applications Infrastructure project?

42. What is the power of the stakeholder?

43. How will reports be created?

44. How big is the gap?

45. Who is managing stakeholder engagement?

46. What opportunities exist to provide communications?

47. Who wants to talk about Security?

48. Is your organization ready for change?

49. What are the major Applications Infrastructure project milestones requiring communications or providing communications opportunities?

50. What & Why?

51. How should employers make voices heard?

1.3 Stakeholder Analysis Matrix: Applications Infrastructure

52. Who will obstruct/hinder the Applications Infrastructure project if they are not involved?

53. Economy - home, abroad?

54. What is the issue at stake?

55. Who influences whom?

56. What is the range you need to look at?

57. What makes a person a stakeholder?

58. Guiding question: what is the issue at stake?

59. Who is most dependent on the resources at stake?

60. Price, value, quality?

61. What do people from other organizations see as your organizations weaknesses?

62. What are the mechanisms of public and social accountability, and how can they be made better?

63. How are the threatened Applications Infrastructure project targets being used?

64. Who has control over whom?

65. Innovative aspects?

66. Advantages of proposition?

67. Where are mitigation costs factored in?

68. How to involve media?

69. Partnerships, agencies, distribution?

70. How do rules, behaviors affect stakes?

71. Morale, commitment, leadership?

2.0 Planning Process Group: Applications Infrastructure

72. To what extent are the visions and actions of the partners consistent or divergent with regard to the program?

73. What are the different approaches to building the WBS?

74. In what way has the program contributed towards the issue culture and development included on the public agenda?

75. Contingency planning. if a risk event occurs, what will you do?

76. Will the products created live up to the necessary quality?

77. How can you tell when you are done?

78. How well do the team follow the chosen processes?

79. Does it make any difference if you are successful?

80. How does activity resource estimation affect activity duration estimation?

81. Are the follow-up indicators relevant and do they meet the quality needed to measure the outputs and outcomes of the Applications Infrastructure project?

82. To what extent has the intervention strategy been adapted to the areas of intervention in which it is being implemented?

83. Do the partners have sufficient financial capacity to keep up the benefits produced by the programme?

84. Product breakdown structure (pbs): what is the Applications Infrastructure project result or product, and how should it look like, what are its parts?

85. Have more efficient (sensitive) and appropriate measures been adopted to respond to the political and socio-cultural problems identified?

86. Is the identification of the problems, inequalities and gaps, with respective causes, clear in the Applications Infrastructure project?

87. How are it Applications Infrastructure projects different?

88. If a task is partitionable, is this a sufficient condition to reduce the Applications Infrastructure project duration?

89. What factors are contributing to progress or delay in the achievement of products and results?

90. What business situation is being addressed?

91. If you are late, will anybody notice?

2.1 Project Management Plan: Applications Infrastructure

92. Do the proposed changes from the Applications Infrastructure project include any significant risks to safety?

93. When is a Applications Infrastructure project management plan created?

94. How well are you able to manage your risk?

95. Who is the Applications Infrastructure project Manager?

96. Development trends and opportunities. What if the positive direction and vision of your organization causes expected trends to change?

97. Is the budget realistic?

98. How can you best help your organization to develop consistent practices in Applications Infrastructure project management planning stages?

99. Is the engineering content at a feasibility level-of-detail, and is it sufficiently complete, to provide an adequate basis for the baseline cost estimate?

100. What happened during the process that you found interesting?

101. How do you manage time?

102. Are there any client staffing expectations?

103. Where does all this information come from?

104. Does the selected plan protect privacy?

105. If the Applications Infrastructure project
is complex or scope is specialized, do you have
appropriate and/or qualified staff available to perform
the tasks?

106. What worked well?

107. Is mitigation authorized or recommended?

108. What would you do differently what did not
work?

109. What are the constraints?

110. Who is the sponsor?

111. Has the selected plan been formulated using cost
effectiveness and incremental analysis techniques?

2.2 Scope Management Plan: Applications Infrastructure

112. Do Applications Infrastructure project managers participating in the Applications Infrastructure project know the Applications Infrastructure projects true status first hand?

113. Are stakeholders aware and supportive of the principles and practices of modern software estimation?

114. Has the Applications Infrastructure project manager been identified?

115. Knowing the health of the Applications Infrastructure project – What is the status?

116. Timeline and milestones?

117. Have stakeholder accountabilities & responsibilities been clearly defined?

118. Have all unresolved risks been documented?

119. How are you planning to maintain the scope baseline and how will you manage scope changes?

120. Have all team members been part of identifying risks?

121. What are the risks that could significantly affect the scope of the Applications Infrastructure project?

122. Is there an on-going process in place to monitor Applications Infrastructure project risks?

123. Have activity relationships and interdependencies within tasks been adequately identified?

124. Are enough systems & user personnel assigned to the Applications Infrastructure project?

125. Who is doing what for whom?

126. Has adequate time for orientation & training of Applications Infrastructure project staff been provided for in relation to technical nature of the application and the experience levels of Applications Infrastructure project personnel?

127. Is there a formal set of procedures supporting Stakeholder Management?

128. Do all stakeholders know how to access this repository and where to find the Applications Infrastructure project documentation?

129. Are trade-offs between accepting the risk and mitigating the risk identified?

130. Have the key functions and capabilities been defined and assigned to each release or iteration?

2.3 Requirements Management Plan: Applications Infrastructure

131. Will you use an assessment of the Applications Infrastructure project environment as a tool to discover risk to the requirements process?

132. How will unresolved questions be handled once approval has been obtained?

133. Who will perform the analysis?

134. What is a problem?

135. Has the requirements team been instructed in the Change Control process?

136. What went wrong?

137. Is it new or replacing an existing business system or process?

138. Controlling Applications Infrastructure project requirements involves monitoring the status of the Applications Infrastructure project requirements and managing changes to the requirements. Who is responsible for monitoring and tracking the Applications Infrastructure project requirements?

139. If it exists, where is it housed?

140. When and how will a requirements baseline be established in this Applications Infrastructure project?

141. Should you include sub-activities?

142. Is stakeholder risk tolerance an important factor for the requirements process in this Applications Infrastructure project?

143. Is any organizational data being used or stored?

144. Did you provide clear and concise specifications?

145. Is the system software (non-operating system) new to the IT Applications Infrastructure project team?

146. Who will finally present the work or product(s) for acceptance?

147. Did you avoid subjective, flowery or non-specific statements?

148. Which hardware or software, related to, or as outcome of the Applications Infrastructure project is new to your organization?

149. Is there formal agreement on who has authority to approve a change in requirements?

150. How will bidders price evaluations be done, by deliverables, phases, or in a big bang?

2.4 Requirements Documentation: Applications Infrastructure

151. Where are business rules being captured?

152. Does the system provide the functions which best support the customers needs?

153. Where do system and software requirements come from, what are sources?

154. How will they be documented / shared?

155. Is new technology needed?

156. What is the risk associated with the technology?

157. What is the risk associated with cost and schedule?

158. What are the attributes of a customer?

159. What images does it conjure?

160. How much testing do you need to do to prove that your system is safe?

161. Are there legal issues?

162. Basic work/business process; high-level, what is being touched?

163. Is the origin of the requirement clearly stated?

164. How to document system requirements?

165. What marketing channels do you want to use: e-mail, letter or sms?

166. What is a show stopper in the requirements?

167. How will the proposed Applications Infrastructure project help?

168. How can you document system requirements?

169. Consistency. are there any requirements conflicts?

170. What is your Elevator Speech?

2.5 Requirements Traceability Matrix: Applications Infrastructure

171. Is there a requirements traceability process in place?

172. How small is small enough?

173. How do you manage scope?

174. Do you have a clear understanding of all subcontracts in place?

175. Why use a WBS?

176. What is the WBS?

177. Will you use a Requirements Traceability Matrix?

178. Why do you manage scope?

179. Describe the process for approving requirements so they can be added to the traceability matrix and Applications Infrastructure project work can be performed. Will the Applications Infrastructure project requirements become approved in writing?

180. What percentage of Applications Infrastructure projects are producing traceability matrices between requirements and other work products?

181. What are the chronologies, contingencies, consequences, criteria?

182. How will it affect the stakeholders personally in career?

2.6 Project Scope Statement: Applications Infrastructure

183. What is the most common tool for helping define the detail?

184. Have you been able to easily identify success criteria and create objective measurements for each of the Applications Infrastructure project scopes goal statements?

185. Has a method and process for requirement tracking been developed?

186. How often will scope changes be reviewed?

187. Relevant - ask yourself can you get there; why are you doing this Applications Infrastructure project?

188. Elements of scope management that deal with concept development ?

189. Are there adequate Applications Infrastructure project control systems?

190. Is there a process (test plans, inspections, reviews) defined for verifying outputs for each task?

191. What went right?

192. Who will you recommend approve the change, and when do you recommend the change reviews occur?

193. Write a brief purpose statement for this Applications Infrastructure project. Include a business justification statement. What is the product of this Applications Infrastructure project?

194. If you were to write a list of what should not be included in the scope statement, what are the things that you would recommend be described as out-of-scope?

195. Will the risk status be reported to management on a regular and frequent basis?

196. Change management vs. change leadership - what is the difference?

197. Which risks does the Applications Infrastructure project focus on?

198. Is the plan for your organization of the Applications Infrastructure project resources adequate?

199. Will the Applications Infrastructure project risks be managed according to the Applications Infrastructure projects risk management process?

200. Was planning completed before the Applications Infrastructure project was initiated?

2.7 Assumption and Constraint Log: Applications Infrastructure

201. Are formal code reviews conducted?

202. Violation trace: why ?

203. What weaknesses do you have?

204. How many Applications Infrastructure project staff does this specific process affect?

205. Is this process still needed?

206. Have all stakeholders been identified?

207. Model-building: what data-analytic strategies are useful when building proportional-hazards models?

208. If it is out of compliance, should the process be amended or should the Plan be amended?

209. What to do at recovery?

210. If appropriate, is the deliverable content consistent with current Applications Infrastructure project documents and in compliance with the Document Management Plan?

211. Are there cosmetic errors that hinder readability and comprehension?

212. Have the scope, objectives, costs, benefits and

impacts been communicated to all involved and/or impacted stakeholders and work groups?

213. Is the process working, and people are not executing in compliance of the process?

214. Are there processes in place to ensure internal consistency between the source code components?

215. Are best practices and metrics employed to identify issues, progress, performance, etc.?

216. Have all involved stakeholders and work groups committed to the Applications Infrastructure project?

217. Are there processes in place to ensure that all the terms and code concepts have been documented consistently?

218. No superfluous information or marketing narrative?

219. Do the requirements meet the standards of correctness, completeness, consistency, accuracy, and readability?

2.8 Work Breakdown Structure: Applications Infrastructure

220. Where does it take place?

221. How will you and your Applications Infrastructure project team define the Applications Infrastructure projects scope and work breakdown structure?

222. How far down?

223. When do you stop?

224. When would you develop a Work Breakdown Structure?

225. How big is a work-package?

226. What is the probability of completing the Applications Infrastructure project in less that xx days?

227. Why is it useful?

228. Is it a change in scope?

229. Do you need another level?

230. Is it still viable?

231. What is the probability that the Applications Infrastructure project duration will exceed xx weeks?

232. Is the work breakdown structure (wbs) defined and is the scope of the Applications Infrastructure project clear with assigned deliverable owners?

233. What has to be done?

234. Can you make it?

235. Why would you develop a Work Breakdown Structure?

236. When does it have to be done?

2.9 WBS Dictionary: Applications Infrastructure

237. Are the contractors estimates of costs at completion reconcilable with cost data reported to us?

238. Appropriate work authorization documents which subdivide the contractual effort and responsibilities, within functional organizations?

239. Is all budget available as management reserve identified and excluded from the performance measurement baseline?

240. Are estimates of costs at completion utilized in determining contract funding requirements and reporting them?

241. Does the contractors system provide for accurate cost accumulation and assignment to control accounts in a manner consistent with the budgets using recognized acceptable costing techniques?

242. The anticipated business volume?

243. Are there procedures for monitoring action items and corrective actions to the point of resolution and are corresponding procedures being followed?

244. Are retroactive changes to direct costs and indirect costs prohibited except for the correction of errors and routine accounting adjustments?

245. Are the procedures for identifying indirect costs to incurring organizations, indirect cost pools, and allocating the costs from the pools to the contracts formally documented?

246. Are material costs reported within the same period as that in which BCWP is earned for that material?

247. Budgets assigned to major functional organizations?

248. Are overhead costs budgets established on a basis consistent with anticipated direct business base?

249. Are current work performance indicators and goals relatable to original goals as modified by contractual changes, replanning, and reprogramming actions?

250. The already stated responsible for overhead performance control of related costs?

251. Do work packages reflect the actual way in which the work will be done and are they meaningful products or management-oriented subdivisions of a higher level element of work?

252. Should you have a test for each code module?

253. Are indirect costs charged to the appropriate indirect pools and incurring organization?

254. Does the cost accumulation system provide for

summarization of indirect costs from the point of allocation to the contract total?

255. Where engineering standards or other internal work measurement systems are used, is there a formal relationship between corresponding values and work package budgets?

2.10 Schedule Management Plan: Applications Infrastructure

256. Has the Applications Infrastructure project manager been identified?

257. Who is responsible for estimating the activity durations?

258. Is the ims development and management approach described?

259. Are risk triggers captured?

260. Are Applications Infrastructure project team members committed fulltime?

261. Will rolling way planning be used?

262. Are target dates established for each milestone deliverable?

263. What date will the task finish?

264. Is there a formal set of procedures supporting Issues Management?

265. Is there a set of procedures defining the scope, procedures, and deliverables defining quality control?

266. Does all Applications Infrastructure project documentation reside in a common repository for easy access?

267. Staffing Requirements?

268. Does the resource management plan include a personnel development plan?

269. What does a valid Schedule look like?

270. Is pert / critical path or equivalent methodology being used?

271. Are Applications Infrastructure project leaders committed to this Applications Infrastructure project full time?

272. Is there any form of automated support for Issues Management?

273. Are there any activities or deliverables being added or gold-plated that could be dropped or scaled back without falling short of the original requirement?

274. Which status reports are received per the Applications Infrastructure project Plan?

275. Has the business need been clearly defined?

2.11 Activity List: Applications Infrastructure

276. How detailed should a Applications Infrastructure project get?

277. How difficult will it be to do specific activities on this Applications Infrastructure project?

278. When do the individual activities need to start and finish?

279. For other activities, how much delay can be tolerated?

280. The wbs is developed as part of a joint planning session. and how do you know that youhave done this right?

281. What is your organizations history in doing similar activities?

282. How much slack is available in the Applications Infrastructure project?

283. Is there anything planned that does not need to be here?

284. Who will perform the work?

285. What are the critical bottleneck activities?

286. Is infrastructure setup part of your Applications

Infrastructure project?

287. How do you determine the late start (LS) for each activity?

288. In what sequence?

289. How should ongoing costs be monitored to try to keep the Applications Infrastructure project within budget?

290. What will be performed?

291. When will the work be performed?

292. What is the probability the Applications Infrastructure project can be completed in xx weeks?

293. What are you counting on?

2.12 Activity Attributes: Applications Infrastructure

294. Were there other ways you could have organized the data to achieve similar results?

295. What is the general pattern here?

296. Resources to accomplish the work?

297. Where else does it apply?

298. Activity: what is Missing?

299. Activity: fair or not fair?

300. Can more resources be added?

301. Have you identified the Activity Leveling Priority code value on each activity?

302. Has management defined a definite timeframe for the turnaround or Applications Infrastructure project window?

303. Would you consider either of corresponding activities an outlier?

304. Have constraints been applied to the start and finish milestones for the phases?

305. How many days do you need to complete the work scope with a limit of X number of resources?

306. Are the required resources available?

307. How many resources do you need to complete the work scope within a limit of X number of days?

308. Can you re-assign any activities to another resource to resolve an over-allocation?

309. Activity: what is In the Bag?

310. Does your organization of the data change its meaning?

2.13 Milestone List: Applications Infrastructure

311. Political effects?

312. What specific improvements did you make to the Applications Infrastructure project proposal since the previous time?

313. Own known vulnerabilities?

314. Environmental effects?

315. How late can the activity finish?

316. Obstacles faced?

317. When will the Applications Infrastructure project be complete?

318. Marketing - reach, distribution, awareness?

319. What are your competitors vulnerabilities?

320. Sustaining internal capabilities?

321. Timescales, deadlines and pressures?

322. Reliability of data, plan predictability?

323. Information and research?

324. What is the market for your technology, product

or service?

325. How soon can the activity start?

326. Competitive advantages?

327. New USPs?

328. Do you foresee any technical risks or developmental challenges?

2.14 Network Diagram: Applications Infrastructure

329. If x is long, what would be the completion time if you break x into two parallel parts of y weeks and z weeks?

330. Are you on time?

331. What controls the start and finish of a job?

332. Where do you schedule uncertainty time?

333. Will crashing x weeks return more in benefits than it costs?

334. How difficult will it be to do specific activities on this Applications Infrastructure project?

335. Exercise: what is the probability that the Applications Infrastructure project duration will exceed xx weeks?

336. If the Applications Infrastructure project network diagram cannot change and you have extra personnel resources, what is the BEST thing to do?

337. What is the lowest cost to complete this Applications Infrastructure project in xx weeks?

338. What activities must occur simultaneously with this activity?

339. Planning: who, how long, what to do?

340. Which type of network diagram allows you to depict four types of dependencies?

341. What are the Major Administrative Issues?

342. Can you calculate the confidence level?

343. What activity must be completed immediately before this activity can start?

344. Are the gantt chart and/or network diagram updated periodically and used to assess the overall Applications Infrastructure project timetable?

345. What are the Key Success Factors?

346. What job or jobs precede it?

2.15 Activity Resource Requirements: Applications Infrastructure

347. When does monitoring begin?

348. Other support in specific areas?

349. What is the Work Plan Standard?

350. How many signatures do you require on a check and does this match what is in your policy and procedures?

351. Which logical relationship does the PDM use most often?

352. What are constraints that you might find during the Human Resource Planning process?

353. Are there unresolved issues that need to be addressed?

354. Why do you do that?

355. Organizational Applicability?

356. Anything else?

357. Time for overtime?

358. Do you use tools like decomposition and rolling-wave planning to produce the activity list and other outputs?

359. How do you handle petty cash?

2.16 Resource Breakdown Structure: Applications Infrastructure

360. What is the number one predictor of a groups productivity?

361. Who is allowed to perform which functions?

362. Who will be used as a Applications Infrastructure project team member?

363. Who needs what information?

364. Why is this important?

365. Why do you do it?

366. Any changes from stakeholders?

367. Goals for the Applications Infrastructure project. What is each stakeholders desired outcome for the Applications Infrastructure project?

368. What defines a successful Applications Infrastructure project?

369. What can you do to improve productivity?

370. How difficult will it be to do specific activities on this Applications Infrastructure project?

371. What is Applications Infrastructure project communication management?

372. Why time management?

373. What is the primary purpose of the human resource plan?

374. When do they need the information?

375. Which resource planning tool provides information on resource responsibility and accountability?

376. The list could probably go on, but, the thing that you would most like to know is, How long & How much?

2.17 Activity Duration Estimates: Applications Infrastructure

377. Given your research into similar classes and the work you think is required for this Applications Infrastructure project, what assumptions, variables, or costs would you change from the information provided above?

378. Calculate the expected duration for an activity that has a most likely time of 3, a pessimistic time of 10, and a optimiztic time of 2?

379. Where do schedules come from?

380. Why is it important to determine activity sequencing on Applications Infrastructure projects?

381. What are the main types of contracts if you do decide to outsource?

382. Is a standard form used to obtain bids and proposals from prospective sellers?

383. Who will be the main sponsor for it?

384. What type of contract was used and why?

385. Do you think many other organizations could apply this methodology, or does each organization need to create its own methodology?

386. Which type of mathematical analysis is being

used?

387. Which is a benefit of an analogous Applications Infrastructure project estimate?

388. Are Applications Infrastructure project records organized, maintained, and assessable by Applications Infrastructure project team members?

389. If the optimiztic estimate for an activity is 12days, and the pessimistic estimate is 18days, what is the standard deviation of this activity?

390. Under corresponding circumstances what would be the best thing to do?

391. Do procedures exist describing how the Applications Infrastructure project scope will be managed?

392. Which frame seemed to be the most important and why?

393. Does a process exist for approving or rejecting changes?

394. Are resource rates available to calculate Applications Infrastructure project costs?

395. Would you rate yourself as being risk-averse, risk-neutral, or risk-seeking?

2.18 Duration Estimating Worksheet: Applications Infrastructure

396. What questions do you have?

397. Science = process: remember the scientific method?

398. Can the Applications Infrastructure project be constructed as planned?

399. What is cost and Applications Infrastructure project cost management?

400. Will the Applications Infrastructure project collaborate with the local community and leverage resources?

401. What is next?

402. Why estimate time and cost?

403. What info is needed?

404. What is the total time required to complete the Applications Infrastructure project if no delays occur?

405. What work will be included in the Applications Infrastructure project?

406. What utility impacts are there?

407. When does your organization expect to be able

to complete it?

408. Is a construction detail attached (to aid in explanation)?

409. Define the work as completely as possible. What work will be included in the Applications Infrastructure project?

410. Small or large Applications Infrastructure project?

411. Value pocket identification & quantification what are value pockets?

412. How should ongoing costs be monitored to try to keep the Applications Infrastructure project within budget?

2.19 Project Schedule: Applications Infrastructure

413. Applications Infrastructure project work estimates Who is managing the work estimate quality of work tasks in the Applications Infrastructure project schedule?

414. Are quality inspections and review activities listed in the Applications Infrastructure project schedule(s)?

415. Are all remaining durations correct?

416. How many levels?

417. Why is this particularly bad?

418. Is there a Schedule Management Plan that establishes the criteria and activities for developing, monitoring and controlling the Applications Infrastructure project schedule?

419. Why do you think schedule issues often cause the most conflicts on Applications Infrastructure projects?

420. How effectively were issues able to be resolved without impacting the Applications Infrastructure project Schedule or Budget?

421. What does that mean?

422. If there are any qualifying green components to

this Applications Infrastructure project, what portion of the total Applications Infrastructure project cost is green?

423. What documents, if any, will the subcontractor provide (eg Applications Infrastructure project schedule, quality plan etc)?

424. Is the structure for tracking the Applications Infrastructure project schedule well defined and assigned to a specific individual?

425. How can you fix it?

426. Are key risk mitigation strategies added to the Applications Infrastructure project schedule?

427. Have all Applications Infrastructure project delays been adequately accounted for, communicated to all stakeholders and adjustments made in overall Applications Infrastructure project schedule?

428. Are procedures defined by which the Applications Infrastructure project schedule may be changed?

429. Why do you need schedules?

2.20 Cost Management Plan: Applications Infrastructure

430. Are corrective actions and variances reported?

431. Is it a Applications Infrastructure project?

432. How relevant is this attribute to this Applications Infrastructure project or audit?

433. Contracting method – what contracting method is to be used for the contracts?

434. Do Applications Infrastructure project teams & team members report on status / activities / progress?

435. Are the key elements of a Applications Infrastructure project Charter present?

436. What would the life cycle costs be?

437. Designated small business reserve?

438. Pareto diagrams, statistical sampling, flow charting or trend analysis used quality monitoring?

439. What is the work breakdown structure for the Applications Infrastructure project?

440. Is the schedule updated on a periodic basis?

441. Has the budget been baselined?

442. Have adequate resources been provided by management to ensure Applications Infrastructure project success?

443. Are all vendor contracts closed out?

444. Has the Applications Infrastructure project scope been baselined?

445. Is there general agreement & acceptance of the current status and progress of the Applications Infrastructure project?

446. Ranged estimates?

447. Is Applications Infrastructure project status reviewed with the steering and executive teams at appropriate intervals?

448. Were stakeholders aware and supportive of the principles and practices of modern software estimation?

2.21 Activity Cost Estimates: Applications Infrastructure

449. How do you treat administrative costs in the activity inventory?

450. What makes a good expected result statement?

451. When do you enter into PPM?

452. What happens if you cannot produce the documentation for the single audit?

453. Can you change your activities?

454. What were things that you did very well and want to do the same again on the next Applications Infrastructure project?

455. How do you do activity recasts?

456. How do you fund change orders?

457. Why do you manage cost?

458. Will you need to provide essential services information about activities?

459. Will you use any tools, such as Applications Infrastructure project management software, to assist in capturing Earned Value metrics?

460. Does the estimator estimate by task or by

person?

461. Where can you get activity reports?

462. Is costing method consistent with study goals?

463. How and when do you enter into Applications Infrastructure project Procurement Management?

464. What is the Applications Infrastructure projects sustainability strategy that will ensure Applications Infrastructure project results will endure or be sustained?

465. What is the activity inventory?

466. What makes a good activity description?

2.22 Cost Estimating Worksheet: Applications Infrastructure

467. What is the purpose of estimating?

468. Identify the timeframe necessary to monitor progress and collect data to determine how the selected measure has changed?

469. Who is best positioned to know and assist in identifying corresponding factors?

470. Can a trend be established from historical performance data on the selected measure and are the criteria for using trend analysis or forecasting methods met?

471. Is the Applications Infrastructure project responsive to community need?

472. Ask: are others positioned to know, are others credible, and will others cooperate?

473. Is it feasible to establish a control group arrangement?

474. What will others want?

475. What happens to any remaining funds not used?

476. What costs are to be estimated?

477. What additional Applications Infrastructure

project(s) could be initiated as a result of this Applications Infrastructure project?

478. What can be included?

479. How will the results be shared and to whom?

480. Does the Applications Infrastructure project provide innovative ways for stakeholders to overcome obstacles or deliver better outcomes?

481. Will the Applications Infrastructure project collaborate with the local community and leverage resources?

482. What is the estimated labor cost today based upon this information?

2.23 Cost Baseline: Applications Infrastructure

483. What do you want to measure ?

484. For what purpose ?

485. Review your risk triggers -have your risks changed?

486. Are you asking management for something as a result of this update?

487. How fast?

488. Is the cr within Applications Infrastructure project scope?

489. What is the reality?

490. Does a process exist for establishing a cost baseline to measure Applications Infrastructure project performance?

491. How accurate do cost estimates need to be?

492. Escalation criteria met?

493. How likely is it to go wrong?

494. What is the most important thing to do next to make your Applications Infrastructure project successful?

495. Who will use corresponding metrics ?

496. Has the documentation relating to operation and maintenance of the product(s) or service(s) been delivered to, and accepted by, operations management?

497. Have the lessons learned been filed with the Applications Infrastructure project Management Office?

498. How concrete were original objectives?

499. Has the actual cost of the Applications Infrastructure project (or Applications Infrastructure project phase) been tallied and compared to the approved budget?

500. How do you manage cost?

2.24 Quality Management Plan: Applications Infrastructure

501. How are changes recorded?

502. Can it be done better?

503. Checking the completeness and appropriateness of the sampling and testing. Were the right locations/samples tested for the right parameters?

504. Is a component/condition present?

505. Have all involved stakeholders and work groups committed to the Applications Infrastructure project?

506. How do you ensure that protocols are up to date?

507. How does your organization design processes to ensure others meet customer and others requirements?

508. Diagrams and tables to account for complex concepts and increase overall readability?

509. Have adequate resources been provided by management to ensure Applications Infrastructure project success?

510. What is the Quality Management Plan?

511. How does your organization determine the requirements and product/service features important

to customers?

512. Is this a Requirement?

513. How does the material compare to a regulatory threshold?

514. How do senior leaders create an environment that encourages learning and innovation?

515. What procedures are used to determine if you use, and the number of split, replicate or duplicate samples taken at a site?

516. Can the requirements be traced to the appropriate components of the solution, as well as test scripts?

517. What is the Difference Between a QMP and QAPP?

518. How do you decide what information needs to be recorded?

519. Have all necessary approvals been obtained?

2.25 Quality Metrics: Applications Infrastructure

520. Which are the right metrics to use?

521. Who is willing to lead?

522. Have risk areas been identified?

523. What are your organizations expectations for its quality Applications Infrastructure project?

524. What metrics do you measure?

525. Who notifies stakeholders of normal and abnormal results?

526. What happens if you get an abnormal result?

527. Product Availability ?

528. What documentation is required?

529. Where is quality now?

530. Do you stratify metrics by product or site?

531. How does one achieve stability?

532. How can the effectiveness of each of the activities be measured?

533. How do you know if everyone is trying to

improve the right things?

534. Is the reporting frequency appropriate?

535. How exactly do you define when differences exist?

536. The metrics–what is being considered?

537. Which report did you use to create the data you are submitting?

538. What forces exist that would cause them to change?

539. Are quality metrics defined?

2.26 Process Improvement Plan: Applications Infrastructure

540. Are there forms and procedures to collect and record the data?

541. Who should prepare the process improvement action plan?

542. Are you meeting the quality standards?

543. How do you manage quality?

544. Have storage and access mechanisms and procedures been determined?

545. How do you measure?

546. Does explicit definition of the measures exist?

547. What is quality and how will you ensure it?

548. Does your process ensure quality?

549. What personnel are the champions for the initiative?

550. What personnel are the sponsors for that initiative?

551. What is the return on investment?

552. Management commitment at all levels?

553. Have the frequency of collection and the points in the process where measurements will be made been determined?

554. What lessons have you learned so far?

555. Purpose of goal: the motive is determined by asking, why do you want to achieve this goal?

556. Are you making progress on the goals?

557. Are you making progress on your improvement plan?

558. Modeling current processes is great, and will you ever see a return on that investment?

2.27 Responsibility Assignment Matrix: Applications Infrastructure

559. Authorization to proceed with all authorized work?

560. Are records maintained to show how management reserves are used?

561. What are the known stakeholder requirements?

562. Identify and isolate causes of favorable and unfavorable cost and schedule variances?

563. Is work properly classified as measured effort, LOE, or apportioned effort and appropriately separated?

564. Do you need to convince people that its well worth the time and effort?

565. Past experience – the person or the group worked at something similar in the past?

566. Who is responsible for work and budgets for each wbs?

567. What are some important Applications Infrastructure project communications management tools?

568. Who is going to do that work?

569. Are there any drawbacks to using a responsibility assignment matrix?

570. What simple tool can you use to help identify and prioritize Applications Infrastructure project risks that is very low tech and high touch?

571. Are detailed work packages planned as far in advance as practicable?

572. What are the deliverables?

573. Is all contract work included in the CWBS?

574. The staff characteristics – is the group or the person capable to work together as a team?

575. Are overhead cost budgets established for each organization which has authority to incur overhead costs?

576. Are authorized changes being incorporated in a timely manner?

2.28 Roles and Responsibilities: Applications Infrastructure

577. Are the quality assurance functions and related roles and responsibilities clearly defined?

578. Implementation of actions: Who are the responsible units?

579. Attainable / achievable: the goal is attainable; can you actually accomplish the goal?

580. What should you highlight for improvement?

581. What are your major roles and responsibilities in the area of performance measurement and assessment?

582. What should you do now to ensure that you are exceeding expectations and excelling in your current position?

583. Key conclusions and recommendations: Are conclusions and recommendations relevant and acceptable?

584. What areas of supervision are challenging for you?

585. Does the team have access to and ability to use data analysis tools?

586. How is your work-life balance?

587. What areas would you highlight for changes or improvements?

588. What specific behaviors did you observe?

589. Do the values and practices inherent in the culture of your organization foster or hinder the process?

590. How well did the Applications Infrastructure project Team understand the expectations of specific roles and responsibilities?

591. Once the responsibilities are defined for the Applications Infrastructure project, have the deliverables, roles and responsibilities been clearly communicated to every participant?

592. Influence: what areas of organizational decision making are you able to influence when you do not have authority to make the final decision?

593. Do you take the time to clearly define roles and responsibilities on Applications Infrastructure project tasks?

594. Is feedback clearly communicated and non-judgmental?

595. What is working well?

2.29 Human Resource Management Plan: Applications Infrastructure

596. List the assumptions made to date. What did you have to assume to be true to complete the charter?

597. How do you determine what key skills and talents are needed to meet the objectives. Is your organization primarily focused on a specific industry?

598. Are cause and effect determined for risks when others occur?

599. Are change requests logged and managed?

600. Does all Applications Infrastructure project documentation reside in a common repository for easy access?

601. Does the Applications Infrastructure project have a Statement of Work?

602. Is the steering committee active in Applications Infrastructure project oversight?

603. Is the Applications Infrastructure project schedule available for all Applications Infrastructure project team members to review?

604. Are risk oriented checklists used during risk identification?

605. Who is involved?

606. Were Applications Infrastructure project team members involved in detailed estimating and scheduling?

607. Are the schedule estimates reasonable given the Applications Infrastructure project?

608. Are decisions captured in a decisions log?

609. Are key risk mitigation strategies added to the Applications Infrastructure project schedule?

610. Was the scope definition used in task sequencing?

611. Do you have the reasons why the changes to your organizational systems and capabilities are required?

612. Are action items captured and managed?

613. Is your organization heading towards expansion, outsourcing of certain talents or making cut-backs to save money?

2.30 Communications Management Plan: Applications Infrastructure

614. Do you feel more overwhelmed by stakeholders?

615. Do you ask; can you recommend others for you to talk with about this initiative?

616. Who did you turn to if you had questions?

617. Are there potential barriers between the team and the stakeholder?

618. Are others part of the communications management plan?

619. Can you think of other people who might have concerns or interests?

620. Who to learn from?

621. Are there too many who have an interest in some aspect of your work?

622. What does the stakeholder need from the team?

623. What is the stakeholders level of authority?

624. What help do you and your team need from the stakeholder?

625. Are you constantly rushing from meeting to meeting?

626. Who have you worked with in past, similar initiatives?

627. How did the term stakeholder originate?

628. Do you then often overlook a key stakeholder or stakeholder group?

629. How do you manage communications?

630. Who is the stakeholder?

631. Are there common objectives between the team and the stakeholder?

632. Are others needed?

633. Do you feel a register helps?

2.31 Risk Management Plan: Applications Infrastructure

634. How will the Applications Infrastructure project know if your organizations risk response actions were effective?

635. How risk averse are you?

636. Should the risk be taken at all?

637. What is the likelihood that your organization would accept responsibility for the risk?

638. Have you worked with the customer in the past?

639. Why do you need to manage Applications Infrastructure project Risk?

640. Maximize short-term return on investment?

641. Can it be changed quickly?

642. What is the likelihood?

643. Degree of confidence in estimated size estimate?

644. Is the process being followed?

645. What are the chances the risk event will occur?

646. Havent software Applications Infrastructure projects been late before?

647. What would you do?

648. Is the technology to be built new to your organization?

649. How is risk response planning performed?

650. Are you on schedule?

651. Are enough people available?

652. Is this an issue, action item, question or a risk?

653. Risks should be identified during which phase of Applications Infrastructure project management life cycle?

2.32 Risk Register: Applications Infrastructure

654. What risks might negatively or positively affect achieving the Applications Infrastructure project objectives?

655. Are there any knock-on effects/impact on any of the other areas?

656. Who needs to know about this?

657. Preventative actions - planned actions to reduce the likelihood a risk will occur and/or reduce the seriousness should it occur. What should you do now?

658. What will be done?

659. When would you develop a risk register?

660. Are corrective measures implemented as planned?

661. What is a Community Risk Register?

662. Recovery actions - planned actions taken once a risk has occurred to allow you to move on. What should you do after?

663. Why would you develop a risk register?

664. Does the evidence highlight any areas to advance opportunities or foster good relations. If yes

what steps will be taken?

665. What is a Risk?

666. What evidence do you have to justify the likelihood score of the risk (audit, incident report, claim, complaints, inspection, internal review)?

667. How is a Community Risk Register created?

668. Are implemented controls working as others should?

669. When will it happen?

670. How are risks identified?

671. Are there any gaps in the evidence?

672. Budget and schedule: what are the estimated costs and schedules for performing risk-related activities?

2.33 Probability and Impact Assessment: Applications Infrastructure

673. Are flexibility and reuse paramount?

674. Can you stabilize dynamic risk factors?

675. Is the customer technically sophisticated in the product area?

676. What will be cost of redeployment of personnel?

677. What is the likely future demand of the customer?

678. What should be the external organizations responsibility vis-à-vis total stake in the Applications Infrastructure project?

679. Are the risk data timely and relevant?

680. How is the risk management process used in practice?

681. Have decisions that should be left open because of inadequate information on technology been identified and responsibility assigned for reducing the uncertainty?

682. What are the tools and techniques used in managing the challenges faced?

683. Will there be an increase in the political conservatism?

684. Management -what contingency plans do you have if the risk becomes a reality?

685. Who should be notified of the occurrence of each of the risk indicators?

686. What should be done with non-critical risks?

687. Who will be in command to monitor and control the performance of the consortium members (consortium leader/client)?

688. What can you do about it?

689. How do you maximize short-term return on investment?

690. What will be the impact or consequence if the risk occurs?

691. What is the likelihood of a breakthrough?

2.34 Probability and Impact Matrix: Applications Infrastructure

692. Could others have been better mitigated?

693. What is the culture of the market and your organization?

694. Is security a central objective?

695. What are the current or emerging trends of culture?

696. During Applications Infrastructure project executing, a team member identifies a risk that is not in the risk register. What should you do?

697. What should be done with risks on the watch list?

698. Which is an input to the risk management process?

699. How well is the risk understood?

700. Who are the owners?

701. How will economic events and trends likely affect the Applications Infrastructure project?

702. During Applications Infrastructure project executing, a major problem occurs that was not included in the risk register. What should you do FIRST?

703. What things might go wrong?

704. Does the software engineering team have the right mix of skills?

705. Workarounds are determined during which step of risk management?

706. What is your anticipated volatility of the requirements?

707. How are the local factors going to affect the absorption?

2.35 Risk Data Sheet: Applications Infrastructure

708. What can you do?

709. Do effective diagnostic tests exist?

710. What is the environment within which you operate (social trends, economic, community values, broad based participation, national directions etc.)?

711. How can it happen?

712. How can hazards be reduced?

713. What are your core values?

714. Has the most cost-effective solution been chosen?

715. During work activities could hazards exist?

716. What are the main threats to your existence?

717. What are you weak at and therefore need to do better?

718. What is the likelihood of it happening?

719. Has a sensitivity analysis been carried out?

720. If it happens, what are the consequences?

721. What were the Causes that contributed?

722. What are you trying to achieve (Objectives)?

723. Will revised controls lead to tolerable risk levels?

724. How reliable is the data source?

725. Who has a vested interest in how you perform as your organization (our stakeholders)?

726. What will be the consequences if it happens?

2.36 Procurement Management Plan: Applications Infrastructure

727. Are written status reports provided on a designated frequent basis?

728. What types of contracts will be used?

729. Has the Applications Infrastructure project scope been baselined?

730. Is quality monitored from the perspective of the customers needs and expectations?

731. Are post milestone Applications Infrastructure project reviews (PMPR) conducted with your organization at least once a year?

732. Is a payment system in place with proper reviews and approvals?

733. Is the Applications Infrastructure project schedule available for all Applications Infrastructure project team members to review?

734. Are governance roles and responsibilities documented?

735. Have all documents been archived in a Applications Infrastructure project repository for each release?

736. Is there an on-going process in place to monitor

Applications Infrastructure project risks?

737. Have the key elements of a coherent Applications Infrastructure project management strategy been established?

738. Is there an issues management plan in place?

739. Are updated Applications Infrastructure project time & resource estimates reasonable based on the current Applications Infrastructure project stage?

740. Are the key elements of a Applications Infrastructure project Charter present?

741. Similar Applications Infrastructure projects?

742. Is the communication plan being followed?

2.37 Source Selection Criteria: Applications Infrastructure

743. How much past performance information should be requested?

744. How organization are proposed quotes/prices?

745. Are evaluators ready to begin this task?

746. What can not be disclosed?

747. When should debriefings be held and how should they be scheduled?

748. What should a DRFP include?

749. Are responses to considerations adequate?

750. Has all proposal data been loaded?

751. How are clarifications and communications appropriately used?

752. What should be the contracting officers strategy?

753. Can you prevent comparison of proposals?

754. Is there collaboration among your evaluators?

755. How will you evaluate offerors proposals?

756. How will you decide an evaluators write up is

sufficient?

757. Who must be notified?

758. What evidence should be provided regarding proposal evaluations?

759. Are resultant proposal revisions allowed?

760. Is the offeror pricing what is technically proposed?

761. What source selection software is your team using?

762. How long will it take for the purchase cost to be the same as the lease cost?

2.38 Stakeholder Management Plan: Applications Infrastructure

763. Have Applications Infrastructure project success criteria been defined?

764. Are multiple estimation methods being employed?

765. Are staff skills known and available for each task?

766. How is information analyzed, and what specific pieces of data would be of interest to the Applications Infrastructure project manager?

767. Is there a Steering Committee in place?

768. Does a documented Applications Infrastructure project organizational policy & plan (i.e. governance model) exist?

769. Are there nonconformance issues?

770. Are changes in deliverable commitments agreed to by all affected groups & individuals?

771. What specific resources will be required for implementation activities?

772. Is the current scope of the Applications Infrastructure project substantially different than that originally defined?

773. Does the Applications Infrastructure project have a formal Applications Infrastructure project Charter?

774. Are tasks tracked by hours?

775. Who is responsible for arranging and managing the review(s)?

776. Has the schedule been baselined?

777. Are there unnecessary steps that are creating bottlenecks and/or causing people to wait?

778. Are the key elements of a Applications Infrastructure project Charter present?

2.39 Change Management Plan: Applications Infrastructure

779. Who will do the training?

780. What relationships will change?

781. What is going to be done differently?

782. Where do you want to be?

783. What time commitment will this involve?

784. Has the priority for this Applications Infrastructure project been set by the Business Unit Management Team?

785. What risks may occur upfront, during implementation and after implementation?

786. Have the systems been configured and tested?

787. How do you gain sponsors buy-in to the communication plan?

788. What risks may occur upfront?

789. Has this been negotiated with the customer and sponsor?

790. When should a given message be communicated?

791. What are the key change management success metrics?

792. Has a training need analysis been carried out?

793. Where will the funds come from?

794. Has an information & communications plan been developed?

795. What new roles are needed?

3.0 Executing Process Group: Applications Infrastructure

796. Mitigate. what will you do to minimize the impact should a risk event occur?

797. Is the schedule for the set products being met?

798. Do Applications Infrastructure project managers understand your organizational context for Applications Infrastructure projects?

799. What does it mean to take a systems view of a Applications Infrastructure project?

800. Will outside resources be needed to help?

801. Will a new application be developed using existing hardware, software, and networks?

802. Are escalated issues resolved promptly?

803. When is the appropriate time to bring the scorecard to Board meetings?

804. Who will provide training?

805. What type of information goes in the quality assurance plan?

806. What are the challenges Applications Infrastructure project teams face?

807. Is the Applications Infrastructure project performing better or worse than planned?

808. It under budget or over budget?

809. Why is it important to determine activity sequencing on Applications Infrastructure projects?

810. What were things that you did very well and want to do the same again on the next Applications Infrastructure project?

811. On which process should team members spend the most time?

812. When will the Applications Infrastructure project be done?

813. What type of people would you want on your team?

814. Is the program supported by national and/or local organizations?

3.1 Team Member Status Report: Applications Infrastructure

815. What is to be done?

816. Does every department have to have a Applications Infrastructure project Manager on staff?

817. Is there evidence that staff is taking a more professional approach toward management of your organizations Applications Infrastructure projects?

818. Are the attitudes of staff regarding Applications Infrastructure project work improving?

819. Does the product, good, or service already exist within your organization?

820. When a teams productivity and success depend on collaboration and the efficient flow of information, what generally fails them?

821. The problem with Reward & Recognition Programs is that the truly deserving people all too often get left out. How can you make it practical?

822. How will resource planning be done?

823. How does this product, good, or service meet the needs of the Applications Infrastructure project and your organization as a whole?

824. Do you have an Enterprise Applications

Infrastructure project Management Office (EPMO)?

825. Are your organizations Applications Infrastructure projects more successful over time?

826. How much risk is involved?

827. Will the staff do training or is that done by a third party?

828. Does your organization have the means (staff, money, contract, etc.) to produce or to acquire the product, good, or service?

829. How can you make it practical?

830. What specific interest groups do you have in place?

831. How it is to be done?

832. Are the products of your organizations Applications Infrastructure projects meeting customers objectives?

833. Why is it to be done?

3.2 Change Request: Applications Infrastructure

834. When to submit a change request?

835. Has a formal technical review been conducted to assess technical correctness?

836. Has the change been highlighted and documented in the CSCI?

837. How many lines of code must be changed to implement the change?

838. Why control change across the life cycle?

839. Will the change use memory to the extent that other functions will be not have sufficient memory to operate effectively?

840. Will all change requests be unconditionally tracked through this process?

841. What mechanism is used to appraise others of changes that are made?

842. How are changes requested (forms, method of communication)?

843. What needs to be communicated?

844. Why do you want to have a change control system?

845. Should staff call into the helpdesk or go to the website?

846. Who can suggest changes?

847. Change request coordination ?

848. Which requirements attributes affect the risk to reliability the most?

849. Are there requirements attributes that can discriminate between high and low reliability?

850. Who is responsible to authorize changes?

851. What can be filed?

852. Who needs to approve change requests?

853. Is it feasible to use requirements attributes as predictors of reliability?

3.3 Change Log: Applications Infrastructure

854. Does the suggested change request represent a desired enhancement to the products functionality?

855. Is the change request within Applications Infrastructure project scope?

856. Will the Applications Infrastructure project fail if the change request is not executed?

857. When was the request submitted?

858. Is the change backward compatible without limitations?

859. How does this change affect the timeline of the schedule?

860. Where do changes come from?

861. How does this change affect scope?

862. Is the requested change request a result of changes in other Applications Infrastructure project(s)?

863. Do the described changes impact on the integrity or security of the system?

864. Is the submitted change a new change or a modification of a previously approved change?

865. How does this relate to the standards developed for specific business processes?

866. Who initiated the change request?

867. Is this a mandatory replacement?

868. When was the request approved?

869. Should a more thorough impact analysis be conducted?

870. Does the suggested change request seem to represent a necessary enhancement to the product?

871. Is the change request open, closed or pending?

3.4 Decision Log: Applications Infrastructure

872. Which variables make a critical difference?

873. Is everything working as expected?

874. With whom was the decision shared or considered?

875. How effective is maintaining the log at facilitating organizational learning?

876. Who is the decisionmaker?

877. Adversarial environment. is your opponent open to a non-traditional workflow, or will it likely challenge anything you do?

878. What makes you different or better than others companies selling the same thing?

879. Do strategies and tactics aimed at less than full control reduce the costs of management or simply shift the cost burden?

880. Decision-making process; how will the team make decisions?

881. How does the use a Decision Support System influence the strategies/tactics or costs?

882. What is your overall strategy for quality control /

quality assurance procedures?

883. How do you know when you are achieving it?

884. How do you define success?

885. At what point in time does loss become unacceptable?

886. How consolidated and comprehensive a story can you tell by capturing currently available incident data in a central location and through a log of key decisions during an incident?

887. It becomes critical to track and periodically revisit both operational effectiveness; Are you noticing all that you need to, and are you interpreting what you see effectively?

888. What is the average size of your matters in an applicable measurement?

889. What are the cost implications?

890. Does anything need to be adjusted?

891. Who will be given a copy of this document and where will it be kept?

3.5 Quality Audit: Applications Infrastructure

892. Health and safety arrangements; stress management workshops. How does your organization know that it provides a safe and healthy environment?

893. How is the Strategic Plan (and other plans) reviewed and revised?

894. How does your organization know that the system for managing its facilities is appropriately effective and constructive?

895. What does an analysis of your organizations staff profile suggest in terms of its planning, and how is this being addressed?

896. How does your organization know that its policy management system is appropriately effective and constructive?

897. Do all staff have the necessary authority and resources to deliver what is expected of them?

898. How does your organization know that its staff embody the core knowledge, skills and characteristics for which it wishes to be recognized?

899. How does your organization know that the research supervision provided to its staff is appropriately effective and constructive?

900. What is the collective experience of the team to be assigned to an audit?

901. Does everyone know what they are supposed to be doing, how and why?

902. How does your organization know that its processes for managing severance are appropriately effective, constructive and fair?

903. How does your organization know that its promotions system is appropriately effective, constructive and fair?

904. How well do you think your organization engages with the outside community?

905. How does your organization ensure that equipment is appropriately maintained and producing valid results?

906. How does the organization know that its system for maintaining and advancing the capabilities of its staff, particularly in relation to the Mission of the organization, is appropriately effective and constructive?

907. What experience do staff have in the type of work that the audit entails?

908. How does your organization know that its management of its ethical responsibilities is appropriately effective and constructive?

909. How does your organization know that its systems for providing high quality consultancy

services to external parties are appropriately effective and constructive?

910. Is progress against the intentions measurable?

911. What are you trying to accomplish with this audit?

3.6 Team Directory: Applications Infrastructure

912. Who should receive information (all stakeholders)?

913. Decisions: what could be done better to improve the quality of the constructed product?

914. When will you produce deliverables?

915. How does the team resolve conflicts and ensure tasks are completed?

916. Decisions: is the most suitable form of contract being used?

917. Timing: when do the effects of communication take place?

918. Who will talk to the customer?

919. Who are your stakeholders (customers, sponsors, end users, team members)?

920. Where should the information be distributed?

921. Who will be the stakeholders on your next Applications Infrastructure project?

922. Where will the product be used and/or delivered or built when appropriate?

923. Why is the work necessary?

924. What are you going to deliver or accomplish?

925. Have you decided when to celebrate the Applications Infrastructure projects completion date?

926. Process decisions: are all start-up, turn over and close out requirements of the contract satisfied?

927. How and in what format should information be presented?

928. How will you accomplish and manage the objectives?

929. Does a Applications Infrastructure project team directory list all resources assigned to the Applications Infrastructure project?

930. Is construction on schedule?

3.7 Team Operating Agreement: Applications Infrastructure

931. To whom do you deliver your services?

932. Do you send out the agenda and meeting materials in advance?

933. Have you set the goals and objectives of the team?

934. Do you call or email participants to ensure understanding, follow-through and commitment to the meeting outcomes?

935. Do you prevent individuals from dominating the meeting?

936. Are there more than two functional areas represented by your team?

937. What are the current caseload numbers in the unit?

938. What resources can be provided for the team in terms of equipment, space, time for training, protected time and space for meetings, and travel allowances?

939. Seconds for members to respond?

940. Do you vary your voice pace, tone and pitch to engage participants and gain involvement?

941. Do you listen for voice tone and word choice to understand the meaning behind words?

942. Has the appropriate access to relevant data and analysis capability been granted?

943. Did you determine the technology methods that best match the messages to be communicated?

944. What is a Virtual Team?

945. Do you determine the meeting length and time of day?

946. Does your team need access to all documents and information at all times?

947. Are there more than two national cultures represented by your team?

948. What is group supervision?

949. Are team roles clearly defined and accepted?

3.8 Team Performance Assessment: Applications Infrastructure

950. How much interpersonal friction is there in your team?

951. To what degree does the teams work approach provide opportunity for members to engage in fact-based problem solving?

952. How do you keep key people outside the group informed about its accomplishments?

953. Where to from here?

954. What makes opportunities more or less obvious?

955. Do you promptly inform members about major developments that may affect them?

956. Social categorization and intergroup behaviour: Does minimal intergroup discrimination make social identity more positive?

957. If you have criticized someones work for method variance in your role as reviewer, what was the circumstance?

958. To what degree will the team adopt a concrete, clearly understood, and agreed-upon approach that will result in achievement of the teams goals?

959. How do you encourage members to learn from

each other?

960. To what degree can the team measure progress against specific goals?

961. To what degree do team members understand one anothers roles and skills?

962. Can familiarity breed backup?

963. To what degree will the team ensure that all members equitably share the work essential to the success of the team?

964. What structural changes have you made or are you preparing to make?

965. If you have received criticism from reviewers that your work suffered from method variance, what was the circumstance?

966. To what degree are sub-teams possible or necessary?

967. To what degree are the teams goals and objectives clear, simple, and measurable?

968. What do you think is the most constructive thing that could be done now to resolve considerations and disputes about method variance?

969. To what degree do team members frequently explore the teams purpose and its implications?

3.9 Team Member Performance Assessment: Applications Infrastructure

970. To what degree is the team cognizant of small wins to be celebrated along the way?

971. To what degree can team members meet frequently enough to accomplish the teams ends?

972. In what areas would you like to concentrate your knowledge and resources?

973. How often are assessments to be conducted?

974. What makes them effective?

975. What kinds of performance factors / elements do you use?

976. For what period of time is a member rated?

977. Should a ratee get a copy of all the raters documents about the employees performance?

978. How are evaluation results utilized?

979. How do you currently use the time that is available?

980. To what degree are the goals realistic?

981. To what degree are the skill areas critical to team

performance present?

982. How accurately is your plan implemented?

983. Does adaptive training work?

984. How should adaptive assessments be implemented?

985. To what degree do all members feel responsible for all agreed-upon measures?

986. What changes do you need to make to align practices with beliefs?

987. Why were corresponding selected?

988. What is the large, desired outcome?

3.10 Issue Log: Applications Infrastructure

989. What is the impact on the risks?

990. Why do you manage communications?

991. What is the stakeholders political influence?

992. What is a change?

993. Do you often overlook a key stakeholder or stakeholder group?

994. Is the issue log kept in a safe place?

995. What effort will a change need?

996. How do you manage human resources?

997. Why multiple evaluators?

998. Are they needed?

999. What are the typical contents?

1000. How often do you engage with stakeholders?

1001. Are the Applications Infrastructure project issues uniquely identified, including to which product they refer?

1002. Do you have members of your team responsible

for certain stakeholders?

1003. Who do you turn to if you have questions?

1004. Is access to the Issue Log controlled?

1005. How much time does it take to do it?

4.0 Monitoring and Controlling Process Group: Applications Infrastructure

1006. How should needs be met?

1007. Is it what was agreed upon?

1008. Specific - is the objective clear in terms of what, how, when, and where the situation will be changed?

1009. Were escalated issues resolved promptly?

1010. Accuracy: what design will lead to accurate information?

1011. What areas were overlooked on this Applications Infrastructure project?

1012. How is agile program management done?

1013. Change, where should you look for problems?

1014. In what way has the program come up with innovative measures for problem-solving?

1015. Did the Applications Infrastructure project team have the right skills?

1016. What resources are necessary?

1017. Is progress on outcomes due to your program?

1018. What is the timeline?

1019. How is Agile Applications Infrastructure project Management done?

1020. What is the timeline for the Applications Infrastructure project?

1021. If action is called for, what form should it take?

4.1 Project Performance Report: Applications Infrastructure

1022. To what degree do members articulate the goals beyond the team membership?

1023. To what degree do team members agree with the goals, relative importance, and the ways in which achievement will be measured?

1024. To what degree will new and supplemental skills be introduced as the need is recognized?

1025. To what degree does the task meet individual needs?

1026. What is the degree to which rules govern information exchange between individuals within your organization?

1027. To what degree does the teams purpose contain themes that are particularly meaningful and memorable?

1028. To what degree are the structures of the formal organization consistent with the behaviors in the informal organization?

1029. To what degree do the structures of the formal organization motivate taskrelevant behavior and facilitate task completion?

1030. How can Applications Infrastructure project

sustainability be maintained?

1031. To what degree do individual skills and abilities match task demands?

1032. To what degree are the demands of the task compatible with and converge with the mission and functions of the formal organization?

1033. To what degree do team members articulate the teams work approach?

1034. How will procurement be coordinated with other Applications Infrastructure project aspects, such as scheduling and performance reporting?

1035. To what degree is there centralized control of information sharing?

1036. To what degree will the approach capitalize on and enhance the skills of all team members in a manner that takes into consideration other demands on members of the team?

1037. What is the degree to which rules govern information exchange between groups?

1038. What is the PRS?

4.2 Variance Analysis: Applications Infrastructure

1039. How are variances affected by multiple material and labor categories?

1040. Are the wbs and organizational levels for application of the Applications Infrastructure projected overhead costs identified?

1041. What is your organizations rationale for sharing expenses and services between business segments?

1042. Budget versus actual. how does the monthly budget compare to actual experience?

1043. Are the bases and rates for allocating costs from each indirect pool consistently applied?

1044. What can be the cause of an increase in costs?

1045. Are indirect costs accumulated for comparison with the corresponding budgets?

1046. Is the anticipated (firm and potential) business base Applications Infrastructure projected in a rational, consistent manner?

1047. What are the direct labor dollars and/or hours?

1048. Are there changes in the direct base to which overhead costs are allocated?

1049. Are there knowledgeable Applications Infrastructure projections of future performance?

1050. Are there quarterly budgets with quarterly performance comparisons?

1051. Is budgeted cost for work performed calculated in a manner consistent with the way work is planned?

1052. Why are standard cost systems used?

1053. What should management do?

1054. How do you manage changes in the nature of the overhead requirements?

1055. At what point should variances be isolated and brought to the attention of the management?

1056. What is the dollar amount of the fluctuation?

4.3 Earned Value Status: Applications Infrastructure

1057. How does this compare with other Applications Infrastructure projects?

1058. Where is evidence-based earned value in your organization reported?

1059. Verification is a process of ensuring that the developed system satisfies the stakeholders agreements and specifications; Are you building the product right? What do you verify?

1060. If earned value management (EVM) is so good in determining the true status of a Applications Infrastructure project and Applications Infrastructure project its completion, why is it that hardly any one uses it in information systems related Applications Infrastructure projects?

1061. Validation is a process of ensuring that the developed system will actually achieve the stakeholders desired outcomes; Are you building the right product? What do you validate?

1062. Are you hitting your Applications Infrastructure projects targets?

1063. What is the unit of forecast value?

1064. Earned value can be used in almost any Applications Infrastructure project situation and in almost any Applications Infrastructure project environment. it may be used on large Applications Infrastructure projects, medium sized Applications Infrastructure projects, tiny Applications Infrastructure projects (in cut-down form), complex and simple Applications Infrastructure projects and in any market sector. some people, of course, know all about earned value, they have used it for years - but perhaps not as effectively as they could have?

1065. How much is it going to cost by the finish?

1066. When is it going to finish?

1067. Where are your problem areas?

4.4 Risk Audit: Applications Infrastructure

1068. What expertise does the Board have on quality, outcomes, and errors?

1069. To what extent are auditors influenced by the business risk assessment in the audit process, and how can auditors create more effective mental models to more fully examine contradictory evidence?

1070. What does your data tell you about your risks?

1071. Are staff committed for the duration of the product?

1072. Will participants be required to sign a legally counselled waiver or risk disclaimer when entering an event?

1073. For this risk .. what do you need to stop doing, start doing and keep doing?

1074. Tradeoff: how much risk can be tolerated and still deliver the products where they need to be?

1075. Is Applications Infrastructure project scope stable?

1076. What are the differences and similarities between strategic and operational risks in your organization?

1077. Where will the next scandal or adverse media involving your organization come from?

1078. Does your organization communicate regularly and effectively with its members?

1079. Is the number of people on the Applications Infrastructure project team adequate to do the job?

1080. What compliance systems do you have in place to address quality, errors, and outcomes?

1081. Does your organization meet the terms of any contracts with which it is involved?

1082. Does your organization have an up-to-date constitution?

1083. Estimated size of product in number of programs, files, transactions?

1084. Do you have proper induction processes for all new paid staff and volunteers who have a specific role and responsibility?

1085. Are testing tools available and suitable?

1086. Is the customer willing to participate in reviews?

1087. Are auditors able to effectively apply more soft evidence found in the risk-assessment process with the results of more tangible audit evidence found through more substantive testing?

4.5 Contractor Status Report: Applications Infrastructure

1088. Are there contractual transfer concerns?

1089. How does the proposed individual meet each requirement?

1090. What process manages the contracts?

1091. What are the minimum and optimal bandwidth requirements for the proposed solution?

1092. If applicable; describe your standard schedule for new software version releases. Are new software version releases included in the standard maintenance plan?

1093. Who can list a Applications Infrastructure project as organization experience, your organization or a previous employee of your organization?

1094. What is the average response time for answering a support call?

1095. How long have you been using the services?

1096. What was the final actual cost?

1097. What was the budget or estimated cost for your organizations services?

1098. What was the actual budget or estimated cost

for your organizations services?

1099. What was the overall budget or estimated cost?

1100. How is risk transferred?

1101. Describe how often regular updates are made to the proposed solution. Are corresponding regular updates included in the standard maintenance plan?

4.6 Formal Acceptance: Applications Infrastructure

1102. How well did the team follow the methodology?

1103. What function(s) does it fill or meet?

1104. Do you perform formal acceptance or burn-in tests?

1105. Was the Applications Infrastructure project goal achieved?

1106. Does it do what Applications Infrastructure project team said it would?

1107. What can you do better next time?

1108. Does it do what client said it would?

1109. Was the Applications Infrastructure project work done on time, within budget, and according to specification?

1110. Do you buy pre-configured systems or build your own configuration?

1111. What lessons were learned about your Applications Infrastructure project management methodology?

1112. What is the Acceptance Management Process?

1113. Is formal acceptance of the Applications Infrastructure project product documented and distributed?

1114. What features, practices, and processes proved to be strengths or weaknesses?

1115. Did the Applications Infrastructure project manager and team act in a professional and ethical manner?

1116. Who would use it?

1117. Was the client satisfied with the Applications Infrastructure project results?

1118. Have all comments been addressed?

1119. General estimate of the costs and times to complete the Applications Infrastructure project?

1120. Was business value realized?

1121. What are the requirements against which to test, Who will execute?

5.0 Closing Process Group: Applications Infrastructure

1122. Is there a clear cause and effect between the activity and the lesson learned?

1123. Did the Applications Infrastructure project team have the right skills?

1124. Just how important is your work to the overall success of the Applications Infrastructure project?

1125. When will the Applications Infrastructure project be done?

1126. What do you need to do?

1127. Were the outcomes different from the already stated planned?

1128. What is an Encumbrance?

1129. What were the desired outcomes?

1130. What level of risk does the proposed budget represent to the Applications Infrastructure project?

1131. Did you do things well?

1132. How well did the team follow the chosen processes?

1133. Will the Applications Infrastructure project

deliverable(s) replace a current asset or group of assets?

1134. Is this a follow-on to a previous Applications Infrastructure project?

1135. What were things that you did very well and want to do the same again on the next Applications Infrastructure project?

1136. How well did the chosen processes produce the expected results?

1137. What could be done to improve the process?

1138. Were cost budgets met?

5.1 Procurement Audit: Applications Infrastructure

1139. Were standards, certifications and evidence required admissible?

1140. Was the pre-qualification screening for issue of tender documents done properly and in a fair manner?

1141. Has your organization fulfilled its obligations related to the payment of social security contributions and taxes?

1142. Is the efficiency of the procurement process regularly evaluated?

1143. Has alternatives been considered for the specified procurement Applications Infrastructure project?

1144. Are internal control systems in place?

1145. Does the approval include approval of prices?

1146. Are there established procedures for dealing with and documenting non-performance and return of goods?

1147. Could bidders learn all relevant information straight from the tender documents?

1148. Were results of the award procedures

published?

1149. Is free and fair (international) competition promoted by organizational policies and legislation, in line with legal, trade organizations and other policies?

1150. Who is verifying the performance of the contract and approving payments?

1151. Does the manual contain policies relating to all business management functions?

1152. Has your organization examined in detail the definition of performance?

1153. Are checks safeguarded against theft, loss, or misuse?

1154. Is there ineffective internal communication in the procurement function/unit?

1155. Did the contracting authority offer unrestricted and full electronic access to the contract documents and any supplementary documents (specifying the internet address in the notice)?

1156. Did additional works amount to no more than 50% of the initial contract?

1157. Are rules in automatic disbursement programs adequate to prevent duplicate payment of invoices?

1158. Was the suitability of candidates accurately assessed?

5.2 Contract Close-Out: Applications Infrastructure

1159. Has each contract been audited to verify acceptance and delivery?

1160. How does it work?

1161. Parties: who is involved?

1162. Are the signers the authorized officials?

1163. How/when used ?

1164. Change in circumstances?

1165. Have all contracts been closed?

1166. Parties: Authorized?

1167. Have all acceptance criteria been met prior to final payment to contractors?

1168. What happens to the recipient of services?

1169. Change in attitude or behavior?

1170. Was the contract type appropriate?

1171. What is capture management?

1172. How is the contracting office notified of the automatic contract close-out?

1173. Have all contracts been completed?

1174. Have all contract records been included in the Applications Infrastructure project archives?

1175. Change in knowledge?

1176. Was the contract complete without requiring numerous changes and revisions?

1177. Was the contract sufficiently clear so as not to result in numerous disputes and misunderstandings?

5.3 Project or Phase Close-Out: Applications Infrastructure

1178. Was the schedule met?

1179. Who is responsible for award close-out?

1180. What are the mandatory communication needs for each stakeholder?

1181. What can you do better next time, and what specific actions can you take to improve?

1182. What benefits or impacts does the stakeholder group expect to obtain as a result of the Applications Infrastructure project?

1183. Does the lesson describe a function that would be done differently the next time?

1184. What are the marketing communication needs for each stakeholder?

1185. What hierarchical authority does the stakeholder have in your organization?

1186. How often did each stakeholder need an update?

1187. What security considerations needed to be addressed during the procurement life cycle?

1188. Who are the Applications Infrastructure project

stakeholders and what are roles and involvement?

1189. Who controlled the resources for the Applications Infrastructure project?

1190. What went well?

1191. Did the Applications Infrastructure project management methodology work?

1192. What was expected from each stakeholder?

1193. Did the delivered product meet the specified requirements and goals of the Applications Infrastructure project?

1194. Is the lesson significant, valid, and applicable?

1195. If you were the Applications Infrastructure project sponsor, how would you determine which Applications Infrastructure project team(s) and/or individuals deserve recognition?

5.4 Lessons Learned: Applications Infrastructure

1196. Does the lesson educate others to improve performance?

1197. How will you allocate your funding resources?

1198. What is the supplier dependency?

1199. Whom to share Lessons Learned Information with?

1200. Was the Applications Infrastructure project manager sufficiently experienced, skilled, trained, supported?

1201. How effective were your design reviews?

1202. How efficient and effective were Applications Infrastructure project team meetings?

1203. How well defined were the acceptance criteria for Applications Infrastructure project deliverables?

1204. How do individuals resolve conflict?

1205. Did the delivered product meet the specified requirements and goals of the Applications Infrastructure project?

1206. What policy constraints are relevant?

1207. What were the main sources of frustration in the Applications Infrastructure project?

1208. What is (are) the indicator(s) of success?

1209. How well were Applications Infrastructure project issues communicated throughout your involvement in the Applications Infrastructure project?

1210. What things surprised you on the Applications Infrastructure project that were not in the plan?

1211. Were the aims and objectives achieved?

1212. Overall, how effective was the performance of the Applications Infrastructure project Manager?

1213. What are the funding priorities for intelligence?

Index

documented   40, 82, 88, 91, 97-98, 100, 138, 142, 149, 153, 207, 211, 219, 251
documents   8, 148, 152, 174, 207, 231, 234, 254-255
dollar   243
dollars   242
domains   89
dominating   230
dormant   108
drawbacks   190
Driver   59
drivers   50, 72
drives   48
driving   108, 111
dropped   156
duplicate   184, 255
duration   4, 134-135, 150, 163, 169, 171, 246
durations   33, 155, 173
during   41, 79, 136, 165, 193, 198, 203-205, 213, 224, 258
dynamic   201
dynamics   38
earlier   122
earned   6, 153, 177, 244-245
easily   146
economic   203, 205
economical   112
Economy   86, 132
edition 9
editorial   1
educate   260
education   19, 97
effect   193, 252
effective   20, 22, 106, 197, 205, 223, 225-227, 234, 246, 260-261
effects 45, 161, 199, 228
efficiency   63, 254
efficient   48, 81, 135, 217, 260
effort   33, 47, 50-51, 120, 152, 189, 236
efforts   32, 80, 130
either   159
electronic   1, 255
element   153
elements   10, 43, 62, 92, 114, 146, 175, 208, 212, 234
Elevator   143

motivation   22, 92
motive 188
moving   103
multiple   211, 236, 242
narrative   149
narrow 69
national   205, 216, 231
nature 139, 243
nearest   12
nearly 105
necessary   61, 64, 68, 86, 107, 118-119, 134, 179, 184, 222, 225, 229, 233, 238
needed   20, 25-27, 41, 65, 67, 93-94, 99, 101, 127, 129, 134, 142, 148, 171, 193, 196, 214-215, 236, 258
negatively   199
negotiate   105
negotiated   104, 213
neither 1
network   3, 163-164
networks   215
Neutral11, 16, 28, 44, 58, 74, 90, 103
normal 100, 185
notice 1, 135, 255
noticing   224
notified   202, 210, 256
notifies 185
number   27, 43, 53, 57, 73, 89, 102, 125, 159-160, 167, 184, 247, 262
numbers   230
numerous   257
objection   21, 25
objective   8, 55, 129, 146, 203, 238
objectives   18, 23-24, 28-29, 37, 67, 91, 93, 105, 112, 116, 148, 182, 193, 196, 199, 206, 218, 229-230, 233, 261
observe   192
observed   77
obsolete   108
obstacles   24, 161, 180
obstruct   132
obtain 105, 169, 258
obtained   40, 140, 184
obtaining   53
obvious   232

CPSIA information can be obtained
at www.ICGtesting.com
Printed in the USA
BVHW041010200819
556236BV00011B/711/P